THE THEME IS BLACKNESS

By the same author

The Theme Is Blackness:

"THE CORNER" AND OTHER PLAYS

Ed Bullins

William Morrow & Company, Inc.
NEW YORK 1973

812.54

B8 7t

10 0890

ajn.1977

Bullins, Ed.
    The theme is Blackness.

    I. Title.
PS3553.U45T5   812'.5'4   72-10199
ISBN 0-688-00012-6
ISBN 0-688-05012-3 (pbk)

        2   3   4   75   74   73

Again to TRIXIE . . .

CONTENTS

I Introduction:

BLACK THEATER: THE '70's — EVOLUTIONARY CHANGES

During the recently left behind '60's, some young Black people in these white, bleak lands imagined the metaphor of the times to be revolution. All were inheritors of a radical Black political and social activist past in America that most were ignorant of, being that they were Black and victims of their oppressors' school system and lack of system for them, members of an alien culture. America's educational institutions are predicated upon keeping Black men ignorant of themselves and the other nonwhite four-fifths of the world. Actually, it is many times a misfortune that Blacks go through these white cultural propaganda mills; places that produce schizoid misfits, properly called Black intellectuals. (Black from their Afros to dark behinds, but at their psychic centers a mortal conflict rages between the Hellenistic Ideal and their *soul.*) Programming for the Black man, the white man's schools are slick job-training centers for induction into the military machine for negroes to become twentieth-century global mercenaries.

A segment of this ill-informed Black youth movement, spurred on by the mass media that fed upon the urban ghetto upheavals of the times, identified themselves with some species of Black Revolutionary Nationalism. A handful of these "revolutionaries" evolved into what can best be described as *Black artists,* using the tired and wasted Western theater form as a medium to effect the most profound changes in Black people here in America, that process termed "altering consciousness," at the same time

[3]

revitalizing the form aesthetically and literally by attacking the intellectual and ideological premises of Western civilization. Their models for future Black conceptualization came through the evolutionary struggle of *creative practice*, and brought about a confrontation with reality that developed into what is now known as *Black theater*.

The Black Revolutionary Nationalist's ideological antecedents reach back to early negro American history, representing the essential conflict among Black thinkers in America—nationalism vs. assimilation. The teachings of the older, traditional nationalist philosophers, fused with contemporary Third World revolutionary thought, became rockbed references of the civil rights and Black Power generation seeking social change through social action, though for the most part remaining unknown in philosophical perspective and not historically understood by the Black youth movement. Some of these intellectual forebears are Booker T. Washington, Marcus Garvey (who initially came to America to study and learn from Booker T.), W. E. B. Du Bois, Richard Wright, Elijah Muhammad, Kwame Nkrumah, Sékou Touré, Frantz Fanon, Chairman Mao; then came Malcolm X, and nothing has been the same since in the Black urban ghetto.

Infused within the Black nationalistic ardor of the young activists were the confused tenets of dated negro radical activism of early twentieth-century America, which has been always Black Nationalism's most hostile adversary within the Black community. Those influenced by the militant integrationist syndrome—the once far left of the negro C.P. membership, the colored trade unionism, protest as practiced historically by the NAACP, the Urban League, CORE, SNCC, and culminating in the reactive rhetoric and revolutionary suicides of Black Panther violent integration (spelled *communalism*)—have traditionally psychologically abhorred and physically hindered most things to do with genuine Black nationhood and self-determination.

[4]

Add to this political misbegotten identity—one having an *emotional* relationship to Blackness but bearing a modern legacy of a surviving leadership which worships the Hellenistic Ideal, whether through G.M., Jane Fonda or Marx—the culturally pervading influence in the ghetto of the Black religionists and Africanists, best examples being the Nation of Islam and the Yoruba tribe of Harlem, and the image of a definite breed of political ghetto cat becomes clearer.

The remainder of the Liberation Movement people affected by politics, philosophy, Black cultural forms and American repression are the Black artists/intellectual activists, the young street niggers, and largest in numbers and the well of Blackness, the Black people people.

All of these elements met, fused, fought and survived in some recognizable form in the strife of the '60's. For poems of actual social and political practice, in hybrid Afro-American style, were being torn from the dark, blood-drenched Dixie nights and the flame-sooted Watts and display case rip-offs of Newarks across this spiritual wasteland, America, and published in obituary columns. And Brothers Malcolm X and Martin Luther King, Jr., held in check the madness and their own murders, for a moment, through threats of retaliatory self-defense and radical nonviolence, in their turns, though Nixon, in the end, clambered across the mounds of made-in-America corpses, to take the seat from where he now pushes buttons marked "Indochina," while ushering impatient, though conservative, Black politicos to the back of "benign neglect."

In the '60's, Black leadership transmitted visions of nationhood. Concrete images, asphalt smooth and stainless as steel, projected the freedom land, coating negro visions, as never before, shuttering the sissy myths of the degenerate end product of Western civilization. And colored people knew they were black, unique, separate, and had a future. For paeans of Blackness were videoed

[5]

throughout Black America, between the stoccado snipe of the assassin's slug, and the Black folk believed, as they are told to do, in the social, political and cultural profundity of that most dramatic of eras. For they then had martyrs as immaculate as Jesus.

But not all the drama then was in the TV slap of a pigstick upside some sister's head in front of an Alabama courthouse, or the *Life* magazine punch of shotgun pellets deflating the heart of a Black thirteen-year-old for the crime of highsidin' among the flames of Burn Baby Burn U.S.A.

No, when the shit went down under the palms on 103rd & Central, there were those of us standing upon a small stage, some miles north of Chief Parker, looking up into bewildered, mostly white faces, explaining why "Clara's Ole Man" might give them some insight as to why the City of Angels was burning that night. And they pleaded ignorance of not understanding the play or why Black people were ready to destroy everything that they cherished, and left soon, to invest in guard dogs, 30-06's and security gates, being the good Americans that they were. (Though the night wasn't entirely wasted: there was enough dough in the box office that night to send bail money to a cousin caught on South Broadway [Watts] with a couch on his back, and to call around about a friend who got busted for burning down a bank, but is now a premed student at U.C.L.A.)

Those were dramatic times that we Black-theater creators set about dramatizing. Black theater then was to be a revolutionary instrument of change. Not only did we have in hand manifestos of Black artistic, aesthetic and cultural revolution, but a body of plays from the visions of the newer Black playwrights: Imamu Baraka (LeRoi Jones), Marvin X, Ben Caldwell, Ron Milner, Jimmie Garrett, Sonia Sanchez and others who have since made some impact upon Black radical aesthetics, and innovations to the Black theatrical form. But more important, in those times of action and activists, when the needs were said to be *relevancy,* in everything, there were emerging theater groups, all a product of their collective place in history, and carrying some germs of Black consciousness and bent on effecting revolutionary change. Black Arts (Harlem), Concept East, Black Arts/ West, The Black House, Spirit House, The Free Southern Theater and The New Lafayette Theater had little to do with or use for predetermined theory or intellectual posturing. Then, as now, the needs of our generation were couched in terms which demanded definite action. Those of us then not playing revolutionary cowboys and pigs, out in the really wild wild West, were touring through Lynchland, Mississippi (as were Roscoe Orman, Gary Bolling and Gilbert Moses, now of The New Lafayette and The Negro Ensemble Company, respectively), or sweating out long, hot summers in store-front theaters in uptight places with names like New Orleans, Detroit, Chicago, Newark and Harlem. As the saying goes, we Black-theater creators, those of us working with and for *the people,* "paid our dues" through revolutionary struggle, by *creative practice.*

In the course of that brief period the still functioning old men of the Black-theater movement—Imamu Baraka, Marvin X, Robert Macbeth and myself—have had collectively and singularly half a dozen theaters shot out from under us (with genuine U.S.-made pistols pointed)—no stage joke here—or lost through ghetto fire. We have already seen the fire next time, dig? So if some of the groups seem unduly close-knit and "parochial" today, there are historical reasons of survival that we have evolved special methods of work and life through social and artistic creative practice.

And my mentioning particular people and groups is not done to play down the efforts of numerous other important theater workers and institutions that presently work from under the Black umbrella, because it's currently

[7]

faddish, but in truth, most of the newer are derivative of their predecessors, or plainly unseasoned, and when some continue to insist upon being designated as *Negro*, in this time of Black consciousness, and on public record as being non- or against nationalism, but can only emotionally relate to America and Europe through some abstract romanticism of a return to a Greco-Romano master-slave ideal, well, one can merely abide by their freakish desires, and wish these brothers well in their existential dilemma.

I have said all this to give the reader some clues as to where I might be coming from, so that my references, alien true, might be somewhat identified, and not completely confuse, for I am concerned with clarifying some images from my hard-earned Black-theater consciousness within this discussion. For I feel that I have some things to communicate.

The reason that critics—Black/white/American—cannot decipher many of the symbols of Black theater is because the artists are consciously migrating to non-Western references. Even while theater, as it is done in America, has models of form and aesthetics found in preindustrial and technological societies, those beginnings are traced from Greece. Black-theater creators, those who have done some *home*work, realize that Greece and the West were civilized by Africans, a superior mingling of cultures from the motherland of humanity, sub-Sahara *Africa*, and that the contemporary Black aesthetics requires that these prototypic sources be exploited, conveyed and translated to *the people* through Black stylistic, symbolic and literal image/renditions. Thus, an innovative strain of Black Art is continually revitalized.

So, the critic, like the Black Western-worshipping intellectual and street-corner revolutionary, comes to Black theater ignorant of the profound heritage that some artists are tapping. These "thinkers," their minds forever damaged by white racism, would believe that contemporary

Black revolutionary theater could provide a matrix for their projected delusions, by weird example, Venus de Milo and Othello copulating in a freaked/out Howard Johnson motel, while shrieking passages from Chairman Mao upon orgasm. What a useless bunch in a people's theater, alienated from the people who are using their instinctive folk/sense to rediscover all that they ever knew from the beginnings of mankind. The most perceptive of this breed that brings its smug mind to Black theater may merely distinguish the exterior edges of a deep dream, while blinded to the interior sense of this altered reality. But there is growth among certain Black, and surprisingly white, critics, which shows that some wish to evolve also with the theater of the immediate future. Though there is a trivial tragedy on the black/side: two Black critics, more accomplished and conceptually endowed than others, are ambivalent concerning whether they will regard Black dramatic criticism seriously and not degenerate into professional press agentry.

Some of the obvious elements that make up the alphabet of the secret language used in Black theater are, naturally, rhythm—black, blues, African; the racial consciousness and subconsciousness of Third World peoples; Black Cultural Nationalism, Black Revolutionary Nationalism and traditional Black people's familial nationalism; dance, as in Black life style and patterns; Black religion in its numerous forms—gospel, negro spiritualism to African spirit, sun, moon, stars and ancestor worship; Black astrology, numerology and symbolism; Black mysticism, magic and myth-science; also, history, fable and legend, vodun ritual-ceremony, Afro-American nigger street styles, and, of course, Black music.

Robert Macbeth, director of The New Lafayette Theatre, needs to be quoted here: ". . . the music, the literature, the architecture and design art, and the art of human movement and singing. When these arts are performed together, in concert, it is called theatre."

When Robert Macbeth and I began talking in the summer of '67 of how to build a Black-theater ensemble company, we committed ourselves to moving away from European references for our art and lives.

Macbeth had read one of my plays in manuscript, sought out my whereabouts, and called me in Oakland, California. I agreed to come east and work with the new theater, The New Lafayette, that he was just starting on a shoestring and hard-borrowed cash, earned by *Black people*.

At that time I was preparing to leave the country. Immediately prior to Macbeth's call I had been working with Eldridge Cleaver, Marvin X, Imamu Baraka (LeRoi Jones), and Sonia Sanchez and numerous other Bay Area revolutionary nationalists in a project we called Black House, a Black cultural-political institution. The political factions fell out with the cultural and artistic members over coalition with white radicals. The Black artists told Cleaver that Black Art and white people do not go together; Cleaver said that Culture is a Gun. He brought in a goon squad to enforce party discipline; in fact, brother was fighting brother. (But in looking back, one can check out the paranoid romanticism, after reading Bakunin's *Revolutionary Catechism*, published in pamphlet form by The Party, under Cleaver's editorship.)

The Black House fell; the Black Revolutionary Artists were the single body able to maintain a community institution of that standard, dedicated to positive community education and cultural-political organization.

So there I was with a dozen finished plays, or more, having a recent history of four theater groups that my plays had built swept away in the Black revolutionary emotionalism and resulting fratricide of the '60's, a fresh score on my rap sheet and a lot of bitterness.

Some of the Black Arts approaches and techniques that Marvin X and I had developed in revolutionary theater and literature workshops on the Coast were brought with me to Harlem when Macbeth sent me a ticket. With Macbeth, a creative genius, providing a strongly structured working situation, building a Black artistic complex from the bottom, teaching the company members and myself from his considerable theater lore, while exercising a creative will to organize thirty talented minds for a collective effort of the highest attainment, The New Lafayette Theatre has evolved to this point in history.

History may define Black theater's social function, but being near the center, I can only believe, like others, that "Black theater's social function is immensely important." Being a past organizer of Black street theater, agit-prop drama, guerrilla theater, and revolutionary Black-theater groups, I realize that we artists did what we could do best, at the time. The activity was part of the *creative practice* of the social and cultural milieu, and conditions must be right for every type of action. It must be right especially for revolution.

Bobby Seale, long interested in the social function of art and media, was an actor in one of the early Black revolutionary theater groups, before he "went for the pig." * (Yes, Bobby played the militant roles.) From working with Bobby as an artist I am unable to believe that he could, psychologically, murder another Black man. I knew him as a natively gifted actor, badly in need of direction, but never a killer, unless defending his family and community. Some crummy politician talked Bobby Seale into jail, plus his own artlessness, and for the lack of values of some revolutionary political hustlers his last role, like Brother Rap's, might be militant martyr.

The conditions must be created for sweeping social and cultural change. It is the Black artist's creative duty to plant, nurture and spread the seeds of change. It is a

* ". . . went *or* go for the pig . . ." is a Black street-language term out of Philly ('50's), meaning "to be *chumped off.*" Neither term included in *Dictionary of Afro-American Slang*, compiled by Clarence Major, International Publishers, New York, 1970.

deadly serious way of life, to make some small contribution in this area of human endeavor, which has an extremely high mortality rate. And there is little chance to contribute to this activity—altering human consciousness —when dead, through revolutionary, reactionary or ritual suicide, except that the work survives and is propagated. In Black theater, this continuity is achieved through *creative struggle:* ruthless dedication in creation of collective forms that will survive any single individual's life.

Working from these premises, then, Black theater becomes a citadel of evolving consciousness. True, this phrase has a noble ring, but that is what certain Black theater creators are about, *to inspire creation of the nation;* the playwrights not excepted.

(To make an open secret more public: in the area of playwrighting, Ed Bullins, at this moment in time, is almost without peer in America—black, white or imported. I admit this, not merely from vanity, but because there is practically no one in America but myself who would dare.

The *20th Century Cycle* is the title given to a group of plays about the lives of some Afro-Americans. When completed, there will be twenty plays in number, each of them individually intended to be fully realized works of art. There is already talk of this collective project surpassing greatness in its scope, though the work is not that astonishing, relative to Bullins' abilities. He has now written more than thirty plays; being a comparatively young artist, there is little reason to believe that he won't easily surpass his early work, in depth of vision and in pure quantity.

Many of Bullins' plays were written for The New Lafayette Theatre because he has worked as a writer to build one of the finest Black community institutions of its kind in the world. Not only has the theater inspired and sustained him as an artist, but with the association of a practicing body of Black artists there has been an untold influence upon his work. His work and The New

Lafayette's cannot be exactly separated or identified. There is no other place, to his knowledge, where a collective entity of Black artistic knowledge, talent, craft, experience and commitment exists. In many ways, The New Lafayette Theatre is the true Black theater.)

The manner that The New Lafayette approaches productions is completely different from those of commercial theater. Commercial Black/white theater would find it physically impossible to achieve what a precision trained ensemble group like The New Lafayette can, though I discover at times a need to see some of my work done elsewhere, and there are many dynamite plays of other Black playwrights the theater is now presenting.

Black theater is part of all theater, whether this fact is liked by Black-theater creators, or denied by ignorant Americans. Black theater's evolution to a visible force in the arts and the cultural life of Black America has changed theater very profoundly, though this change is not yet immediately evident to the white theatergoer.

For one, in Black theater the audience is different. This audience contains all the elements that will create the revolutionary changes among Black people of the near future. This difference causes the audience to have separate needs, desires and behavior. And two, for this audience the material must be original and innovative. Because of these differences the criteria of what encompasses theater is radically altered in America.

In speaking of some Black playwrights, from where Black theater begins: Imamu Baraka has already received my full regard and respect; J. E. Gaines is the best playwright I know; watch Richard Wesley; Melvin Van Peebles is boss; Charles Gordone is separated from reality; Lonne Elder III can, perhaps, quietly disappear with grace; Lorraine Hansberry preceded contemporary Black theater, which isn't negative at all, merely fact; Ron Milner needs to write some more plays; Jimmy Garrett, likewise; Jennie Franklin is a queen; Sonia 15X, Martie

Charles and Adrienne Kennedy are the revolution; and Douglas Turner Ward has my fondest hopes as an all-round theater man—from providing home bases for Black talents such as Gilbert Moses and Michael Schultz, and providing Derek Walcott's inspiring *Dream on Monkey Mountain* with an excellent production, Brother Ward's *creative practice* is evolving in the Blackest sense.

A few other Black artists that interest me: I have spoken of Robert Macbeth—though accused of acting like The God of Black Theater, in truth, he is nothing but its Master, for all of its elements are under his control. There's no male actor working anywhere finer than Sonny Jim—his voice alone would rupture most white actors, if any dared to step upon the same stage with him. And Whitman Mayo is almost unequaled in the variety of things he can do upon stage. There are others, but I shall leave them for the future, if I should have reason to introduce another book in this manner.

The work in this collection was created over the past five-year period (1965–70), and is a chronicle, of sorts, a working model for Black-theater creators, a testimony of an artist investigating his craft, and of a human odyssey of one Black man through the social, political, artistic and cultural Black consciousness of the times.

The future of Black theater will be in its evolution into a profound instrument of altering the slave mentality of Black Americans. In an evil, white world of ever shifting values and reality, for the Black man there must be a sanctuary for re-creation of the Black spirit and African identity. In racist, madmen America, the Black theater has carved out this part of the future for itself. If all around us are losing their heads (spilled out by assassins on Harlem intersections, for some), it may be provident for the Black artist to attempt to hold onto his own, which is a conservative impulse, true, but radical in terms of heretical viewpoints. Political theorists of the Black Arts are confused and disappointing. They sloganeer that Art and Politics Should Be Identical—be serious! Today's politics are the politics of the pig: to murder all dissent and opposition. Black Art is to express what is best in us and for us Black people. Like the people, the people's art and artists have forever survived any opportunistic political expediency of some Fat Mouthin' leader. Black theater is not a Theater of the Lip, as is the style of Black/white hustling America, but a people's theater, dedicated to the continuing survival of Black people. And the artists will continue to evolve with the people, swim within their mass, and emerge through creation after creation. For we know: "The dogs may bark but the caravan passes on."

ED BULLINS

Summer, 1972

DIALECT DETERMINISM

(or The Rally)

THE PEOPLE

BOSS BROTHER
THE VISITOR
THE DOORMAN
LOUD BROTHER
FIRST BROTHER
SECOND BROTHER
YOUNG SISTER
FAT SISTER
SPIRIT OF MALCOLM X
OLD SISTER
GOOD SISTER
THE SERENE MAN

Dialect Determinism (or The Rally) was originally published in *Ante* (Los Angeles: 1966). *This play was first performed at the Firehouse Repertory Theater in San Francisco on August 5, 1965. It was produced by the San Francisco Drama Circle and directed by Robert Hartman. The sets were designed by Louie Gelwicks and Peter Rounds. Lighting was by Verne Shreve.*

The cast members and their roles are as follows:

BOSS BROTHER	MACK MC COY
THE VISITOR	JAMES ROBINSON
THE DOORMAN	JERRY KEMP
LOUD BROTHER	RAY ASHBY

FIRST BROTHER	DOYLE RICHMOND
SECOND BROTHER	ROY HAMMOND
YOUNG SISTER	BLANCHE RICHARDSON
FAT SISTER	MARIE BELL
SPIRIT OF MALCOLM X	MARCUS PERRY
OLD SISTER	DOROTHY PARRISH
GOOD SISTER	MARGO NORMAN
THE SERENE MAN	VOICE OF MACK MC COY

As the curtain rises, negro gospel music plays in an absurd style. A spotlight remains on BOSS BROTHER throughout most of the production, even when HE is not in the central action; however, it diminishes in intensity and alters colors to express mood changes.

BOSS BROTHER stands upon a raised platform or a soap box on the left stage apron, midway between rows of folding chairs on the stage and the theater audience. The first row in the audience is part of the stage set, and BOSS BROTHER will speak in both directions; HE wears a black wooly wig and a dark, conservative business suit. HE arranges papers upon the podium, beside a blackboard.

The BROTHERS and SISTERS file in from stage right and take seats, the MEN on one side, the WOMEN on the other. When all the seats are taken except for the one THE VISITOR will sit in, the remaining BROTHERS and SISTERS file off the stage and fill in the front row. The MEN wear green business suits, purple shirts and orange ties; the WOMEN wear chic shifts of exotic patterns; tropical birds rustle amid purple foliage, across black shoulders, with grape leaves mottling azure and scarlet backgrounds.

The backdrop is an enormous likeness of THE SERENE MAN: in fact, it is a huge, stylized representation of an African mask. The word PEACE is painted and displayed over the entire stage. The word is stenciled upon the backs of

[19]

each chair, and some of the MEN *have the word sewed to the seats of their trousers.*

THE DOORMAN *does not take a seat but walks to the edge of the stage and begins patrolling the length of the stage in a semi-goose step, much in the manner of an automaton.* HE *marches back to the entrance as* BOSS BROTHER *clears his throat and rattles his papers. From beneath a table which stands outside the entrance,* THE DOORMAN *takes a large picture of* THE SERENE MAN *and sets it upon the table.*

The BROTHERS *and* SISTERS *moan and hum to the weird music, and from below the podium* BOSS BROTHER *withdraws a silver pitcher and pours a glass of pink lemonade into a tall glass, takes a drink and swishes the beverage about in his mouth before* HE *pulls back his head and swallows.*

A loud knocking sounds. Only THE DOORMAN *notices.* HE *peers through the entrance as if* HE *were looking through a peephole. (The door is imaginary.)*

THE VISITOR

> *(From outside)*

Good evening!

> (THE DOORMAN *makes motion of cracking door and allows* THE VISITOR *to slip inside. A slamming noise is heard as* THE DOORMAN *shuts the imaginary door.* BOSS BROTHER *jumps slightly at the sound and begins his speech)*

BOSS BROTHER

> *(Mumbles)*

We have come here, Brothers and Sisters, for a great

purpose . . . haaaruump . . . ahh . . . yeah . . . Let us commune.

> (BOSS BROTHER, BROTHERS *and* SISTERS *bow their heads and moan and groan*)

THE DOORMAN

(To THE VISITOR*)*

Evening, Brother!

> (HE *shoves* THE VISITOR *against a wall, having him stretch forward so that* HE *can frisk him*)

BOSS BROTHER

Let us commune in our hour of want, Brothers and Sisters.

THE DOORMAN

First time here?

> (THE VISITOR *nods, bumping his forehead against the backdrop*)

If you'll just let me . . .

> (HE *frisks* THE VISITOR *expertly*)

Will you please empty your pockets out on that table?

> (THE VISITOR *takes out wallet, cards, currency and miscellaneous items from pockets.*
>
> *Places items in manila envelope*)

Now, I'll have to take these things. You'll get these back right after the meeting.

THE VISITOR

How?

THE DOORMAN

Because you are number one, brother.

(Points)

Inside, please.

(The BROTHERS' *and* SISTERS' *eyes fasten upon* THE VISITOR *as* HE *walks to his seat, but* THEY *immediately return to meditation as* BOSS BROTHER *clears his throat)*

BOSS BROTHER

(Croons and puts aside his papers)

I call you Brothers for we have a common experience and we shall share a common future, for we have common aspirations and common destinies . . . as I've mentioned, so if our fates are shared, then we form a brotherhood, or for those of you who shun the unpleasantness you may find in this word, brotherhood, we will only say that we are here for mutual benefits . . . Brothers . . . ha ha ha.

*(*BOSS BROTHER's *movements are slow and flashy.* HE *uses a large white handkerchief to dab his puffy lips and to mop his forehead;* HE *waves the handkerchief like a banner whenever the* CROWD *becomes excited)*

You see it doesn't hurt to be identified with your own, I mean . . . it's not half as bad as some of you newer ones might suspect.

(His eyes seek out THE VISITOR*)*

LOUD BROTHER

(Shouting to BOSS BROTHER*)*

TELL US ABOUT IT, BROTHER, TALK ABOUT IT!

VOICES

Yeah, bring it on down front, man.

Yaasss . . . I see what you means, children.

LOUD BROTHER
GIVE US THE WORD, BROTHER!

VOICES
Yes, the word!

(A spot focuses upon the picture of THE SERENE MAN *and* BOSS BROTHER'S *spot vacillates as the tempo alters)*

BOSS BROTHER
(Smiling)

Well, you know that nationalism ain't an invention of bro— Oh, sorry, I means of the Black man . . . yawhl.

FIRST BROTHER
What yawhl say?

SECOND BROTHER
Let Brother speak!

BOSS BROTHER
It was with the rise of the European nation-states that nationalism becomes evident in history . . .

LOUD BROTHER
That's right!

YOUNG SISTER
It is! Can't you hear those big words he's using? He's got to be right.

FIRST BROTHER
Right!

LOUD BROTHER
THAT'S RIGHT!

SECOND BROTHER

Right!

VOICES

SNO NUF!

(BOSS BROTHER *flutters his handkerchief and drinks his lemonade. The* CROWD *sways with the wonder of the* SPEAKER; *it is an inner rhythm rushing up to their heads from their stirring seats, to smash out in explosive enthusiasm. Sitting still,* THE VISITOR *pulls his eyes away from the* SPEAKER's *and focuses upon his feet)*

BOSS BROTHER

Now in unity we have found by looking at history there is strength . . . in brotherhood there is power, and all we want is power, don't we's, just like everybody else? . . . So as de most honest people on de face of the earth we don't have to fool ourselves by sayin' it's some sort of holy crusade or just fairness if we get our chance finally to kick the hell out of somebody else for a change . . .

FIRST BROTHER

Teach, brother.

SECOND BROTHER

THAT'S RIGHT! BRING IT ON DOWN FRONT, BROTHER!

FAT SISTER

Right! . . . We's de most honest folks . . . history proves dat.

[24]

(After hesitation)

Now, brothers and mah good sisters, now are we really honest?

(Before HE *is answered)*

Nawh, we are no more honest den other humans, for dishonesty is a human trait. AIN'T IT! And ain't we humans?

VOICES

THAT'S RIGHT! THAT'S RIGHT! WE'S HUMAN, AIN'T WE'S!

YOUNG SISTER

Teach, teach, teach, brother.

(With the white handkerchief at his forehead, the SPEAKER *stares out at the* NEW MAN *as* HE *raises his eyes from the floor.* THE VISITOR *begins trembling)*

BOSS BROTHER
(Winks, speaks)

The reason we's don't have to worry 'bout honesty is because dis ain't our society no way and what's ain't yours you don't have to care about no way . . .

LOUD BROTHER
(Stands in his chair, exhorting BOSS BROTHER*)*

THAT'S RIGHT! THAT'S RIGHT! WHAT WE'S HERE FO IS TO GET THE FACTS, THE TRUTH AND NOTHIN' BUT!

FIRST BROTHER

Shut up, man, let Boss Brother talk!

SECOND BROTHER

Yeah, let us hear the word.

(LOUD BROTHER *glares about the stage and takes his seat.* BOSS BROTHER's *eyes scan the stage and the audience like a hypnotist's and* THE VISITOR *shows distress*)

BOSS BROTHER

(Confidentially)

Now let me tell you something you might not have guessed before. You might not have known it but dis ain't America in the Sixties.

LOUD BROTHER

What you say, brother?

BOSS BROTHER

YOU WANTED THE TRUTH, SO I'M TELLIN' YOU THAT DIS AIN'T AMERICA YOU'S IN . . . RIGHT?

FIRST BROTHER

That's what you said, brother. That's what you said.

BOSS BROTHER

Yaasss . . . now this is really Germany . . . the Germany of the late Twenties and Thirties . . . right?

LOUD BROTHER

Nawh, brother, nawh, man. We ain't gonna go fo dat.

BOSS BROTHER

(Disarmingly)

But, brother, you want the truth, so I am confessing dat I'm Hitler . . . right?

VOICES

NO! NO! WE AIN'T GOIN' FO DAT!

BOSS BROTHER

Ain't I's Hitler?

LOUD BROTHER

(Smugly)

Nawh, yawh not no Hitler.

FAT SISTER

Maybe he's tellin' the truth. I always wondered what happened to Hitler.

THE VISITOR

(Rises and challenges BOSS BROTHER*)*

Yawhl jivin' . . . yawhl shuckin'.

(With a flick of his handkerchief BOSS BROTHER *slams* THE VISITOR *back into his seat. As the lights dim momentarily,* BOSS BROTHER *dons a Storm Trooper's jacket and applies a Hitler moustache as the* BROTHERS *and* SISTERS *placidly look on)*

BOSS BROTHER

And I told everyone I had a book coming out . . . you don't know whether I have a book coming out . . . right?

VOICES

RIGHT!

BOSS BROTHER

(Straight-arm salute)

SING RIGHT!

VOICES

RIGHT!!!

BOSS BROTHER

(Strong dialect)

Sho nuf!

[27]

(THE VISITOR *whimpers and trembles, but his sounds are ignored*)

Ha ha ha . . . but comrades, I am really Marx . . . right?

LOUD BROTHER
(Dismayed)

Wrong!

BOSS BROTHER

SING RIGHT!!!

VOICES

WRONG!!!

BOSS BROTHER
(Rejoicing)

YAWHL RIGHT? BROTHERS . . . HA HA HA . . .
For I don't really knows that dere are only nine card-carryin' members in the L.A. cell . . . do I's . . . or are dere ten . . . or two hundred and fifty-eight?

(The light on the SPEAKER becomes hazy and waxes and wanes as it changes hue)

LOUD BROTHER
(Pointing)

YAWHL HEAR DAT? . . . HE'S ONE OF DEM REDS!

BOSS BROTHER

WOULDN'T YAWHL WANT TO BE A FIRST-CLASS COMMUNIST DEN A SECOND-CLASS CITIZEN?

FIRST BROTHER

Nawhl.

SECOND BROTHER

Yeah, man.

VOICES

(In flurries among themselves)

He said first-class!

LOUD BROTHER

I don't want ta be no mahthafukkin' Communist . . . I's a good American.

YOUNG SISTER

Shut up, Tom!

BOSS BROTHER

Don't intimidate the young man . . . and get ahold of yourselves, folks . . . cause I got news for you. Now what's our password?

VOICES

ILLOGIC!

BOSS BROTHER

YAASSS . . . CHILDREN . . . and fo dat I'll confess dat I'm really an impostor . . . I's really Malcolm X . . . BLOODS . . .

> (BOSS BROTHER *has removed his uniform and wig and puts on horn-rimmed glasses and wipes his shaven head)*

SPIRIT OF MALCOLM X

(HE stands from his seat in the middle of the audience and heads for the stage)

THAT'S AN OUTRIGHT SLANDEROUS LIE PUT IN YOUR MOUTH BY BLUE-EYED WHITE DEVILS!

(The SPIRIT is dressed in black suit and red tie)

[29]

(ALL *the* BROTHERS *stand to block the* INVADER *who rushes down the center aisle through the* BROTHERS *and* SISTERS *who were sitting in the front seats but who rise and give the* APPARITION *chase. The* SPIRIT *leaps upon the stage. The* BROTHERS *on stage encircle it as* BOSS BROTHER *tries to crawl under his podium, and* THE VISITOR *huddles within the ranks of* WOMEN *who scream encouragement to the* BROTHERS)

LOUD BROTHER
(Rushes up to the SPIRIT *but remains out of reach)*

I's a killer, a mangler, a mad dog when I's gets started. I's so bad I's have to hold myself back.

(Shakes his fist)

You better be careful, boy!

(The BROTHERS *have taken karate stances.* LOUD BROTHER *finally goes back to the* CROWD *and pushes* FIRST BROTHER *within the* SPIRIT's *reach. The* SPIRIT *breaks* FIRST BROTHER's *neck, backbone and hipbone with a nifty judo chop, and a terrific brawl ensues where the* SPIRIT *disables over half of the* BROTHERS *before* HE *is dragged outside)*

LOUD BROTHER
(From the sidelines)

Liar!

FIRST BROTHER
(Being mauled)

Peace, brother.

SECOND BROTHER
(Gets in a lick)

Fraud.

SPIRIT
(Retaliates)

Take that, brother.

YOUNG SISTER
(In CROWD*)*

Mahthafukker!

VOICES

Teach da truth!

LOUD BROTHER
(To audience as the SPIRIT *is taken off)*

He better not come back or I'll whup him so bad his mama won't take him in.

BOSS BROTHER
(Peers from his hiding place and sees that all is clear)

I'm glad that cowardly dog is gone.

(HE *has rows of ribbons displayed upon his chest)*

To attempt to smear my good name . . . the idea.

FIRST BROTHER
(Returns in bandages and on crutches)

Hush up . . .

(To boasting BROTHERS*)*

so we can hear de word.

Yeah, hush on up!

See, now that order has been gotten at the expense of a few, I can positively say that I am Lenin, right, for he came before Stalin, so I am my own Second Coming, right?

Woweee . . . listen to him . . . he knows everybody.

Then he must be everybody!

(THE VISITOR *moans and* MANY HEADS *turn*)

(To BOSS BROTHER*)*

Hush up yo lyin' mouf, man!

(In time with a blinding flash of light)

But, sister, ain't you never seen me befo? . . .

(An explosion takes place under the SPEAKER's *platform, causing a cloud to rise about him)*

(Cowering)

Nawh . . . I ain't never seen no nothin' like you before.

(The spot on BOSS BROTHER *dims gradually and the one on the likeness of* THE SERENE MAN *brightens)*

Well, I've been away for quite some time, honey. You see, I's really the Wandering Jew.

[32]

LOUD BROTHER
The Wandering Who?

BOSS BROTHER
(As lights change color)

Don't yawhl knows I's Martin Luther, Butterbeans without Susie. That I's Uncle Tom, Fred Schwarz, Emperor Goldwater, Lumumba, Castro, all the L.B.J.'s, Lincoln Rockwell, the Birds' Turds resurrected . . . chickenshit, ya hip?

LOUD BROTHER
Teach, brother.

FIRST BROTHER
THAT'S RIGHT!

SECOND BROTHER
Sho nuf . . . dat's where it's at.

BOSS BROTHER
And in all my glory . . . I's de greatest.

LOUD BROTHER
(Staggering and screaming)
THAT'S RIGHT!

YOUNG SISTER
(Emotionally)

Teach, brother . . . speak the word, the word, the word!

BOSS BROTHER
Very well, I'll give you more, everything and whatever you wish to hear.

FIRST BROTHER
Give it to us, brother.

[33]

YOUNG SISTER
Teach . . . teach . . . teach, brother.

FAT SISTER
The Word, the Word, the Word.

(All lights blacken except for the spot focused upon the picture of THE SERENE MAN)

THE SERENE MAN
(Voice of BOSS BROTHER)

I'S DE GREATEST . . . I'S DE ONE AND ONLY WHO WILL HIP YA TO DIS, BROTHERS! THERE'S AH MESSIAH ON EVERY CORNER! . . . 'N' WE'RE ALL OUT HERE TO FUCK YA . . . BROTHERS!

LOUD BROTHER
(As lights go up)

THE TRUTH! THE FINAL TRUTH!

(HE throws back his head and wails)

FAT SISTER
(Frenzied ecstasy)

Aaaa wooo ouwwalll weesss wa booogie blues in de alley soul so much soul so soulful, lawdy, yes, indeedy, yawhl.

BOSS BROTHER
(Appears in his original clothes)

Now, yawhl knows dat I's goin' to take ov'va, so let me tell ya how's I's goin' to do it so you can help me.

(HE walks to the blackboard and in bright chalk writes large letters, then reads them aloud:)

DIALECT DETERMINISM . . . YAWHL!

(Rustles stir within the BROTHERS' and SISTERS' ranks

[34]

*and grunts of cleared throats are mingled with the
squawks of parrots and farts of zebras)*

FIRST BROTHER

Dialect . . . what's dat?

SECOND BROTHER

Ummmmmmmm . . . ???

BOSS BROTHER

REMEMBER THOSE WORDS, BROTHER.

VOICES

We'll remember.

BOSS BROTHER

Now, to bind us closer together we needs a martyr.

LOUD BROTHER

YEAH, DAT'S WHAT WE NEEDS IS A MARTYR!

FIRST BROTHER
        (To LOUD BROTHER*)*

Say, what's dat?

> *(Eyes search throughout the room, under seats, in
> pockets and purses, to* THE VISITOR *drying his eyes.*
> HE *shakes his head and stares toward* YOUNG SISTER*,
> who stands straightening her nose.* SHE *looks charm-
> ing in her shift)*

YOUNG SISTER
        (Sees all eyes upon her)

Don't look at me
        (Ridiculous)

. . Brothers and sisters . . .

> *(*SHE *turns and stares at* BOSS BROTHER*)*

BOSS BROTHER
(Finds all eyes upon him)

RIGHT!

VOICES

RIGHT!!!

(The BROTHERS *and* SISTERS *surge upon the stage.* THE VISITOR, *the* YOUNG SISTER *and* THE DOORMAN *remain in their places)*

BOSS BROTHER
(Salutes as HE *is stomped)*

SING RIGHT!!!

VOICES
(The GROUP *tears at* BOSS BROTHER *like carrion)*

RIGHT!!!

LOUD BROTHER

I'll get the rope.

*(*HE *rushes to* THE DOORMAN *who hands him the rope and returns to the* MOB. *After* LOUD BROTHER *receives the rope,* THE VISITOR *accepts his personal items.* HE *talks in a whisper to the* YOUNG SISTER *who has wandered over and is giggling)*

THE DOORMAN

Come again, brother.

THE VISITOR

I'll try.

(Sound of the MOB *as* THEY *part to show* LOUD BROTHER *garroting* BOSS BROTHER)*

THE DOORMAN

Never seen my people in such high spirits. Well, good night, brother. Good night, sister. Peace be with you.

(HE *about-faces and begins his patrol*)

THE VISITOR

(With YOUNG SISTER *on his arm)*

And Peace remain with you . . . brother.

(HE *looks at the image of* THE SERENE MAN *and at the* DOORMAN's *back, then leads* YOUNG SISTER *away)*

CURTAIN

IT HAS NO CHOICE

You do not need to leave your room. Remain sitting at your table and listen, simply wait. Do not even wait, be quite still and solitary. The world will freely offer itself to you to be unmasked, it has no choice, it will roll in ecstasy at your feet.

                                                    Franz Kafka

THE PEOPLE

GRACE
STEVE

IT HAS NO CHOICE *was first performed at the Black Arts/ West Repertory Theater/School in San Francisco in Spring, 1966. It was directed by Hillery L. Broadous.*

The cast members and their roles are as follows:

GRACE   JUDY PERKINS
STEVE   HILLERY L. BROADOUS

The bedroom of an apartment unit in Southern California. Unit, meaning in this circumstance, a small, bungalow-like building behind a larger apartment building. The unit has a small kitchen and a bath, and GRACE's *bedroom serves as the front room also.*

In the eighty-degree weather, GRACE *and* STEVE *sprawl in*

*negligee and pajamas upon pastel sheets with the covers
thrown back. Upon the floor, encircling the bed, is the
evidence of a leisurely morning: milk and juice cartons,
coffee cups, a percolator and toaster plugged into a wall
socket, plates, ashtrays and Sunday papers. A radio plays
restful music.*

GRACE *snuggles up to* STEVE *and blows into his ear, break-
ing his nap.*

GRACE
(Bubbling and winding her legs about his torso)

It's been a wonderful holiday, hasn't it, Steve?

STEVE
(Drowsy)

Yeah, baby.

GRACE

But don't you think this has been one of the best holidays
you've ever spent?

STEVE

Yeah. It really has.

(HE *kisses her and begins to roll over but* SHE *curls
from under him)*

GRACE

Since Christmas I've been in some sort'a dream that you've
spun for me, Steve. Are you the Sandman?

STEVE
(Languid)

Nawh . . . baby . . . I'm the boogie man.

GRACE

(Continuing)

I didn't know that life could be so wonderful.

> (STEVE *rises to his elbows and looks at her for a long moment, then* HE *puts out his hand, almost testing if* HE *can touch her, then finding that* HE *can, pulls her to him and kisses her)*

STEVE

(When THEY *break their embrace)*

Christmas couldn't have been better for me either.

GRACE

Yes, just think of what I've been missing for so long.

STEVE

(Naïvely)

I tried to tell you a long time ago that I was the man for you.

GRACE

(Sighing)

Yes, you did, you old bully. But I was too scared of you to find out.

STEVE

(Chuckles)

Scared?

GRACE

Yes, you seemed so serious, Steve.

STEVE

(Disarming)

Well, Grace, I am, ya know. I bet you've never met any-one as serious as me.

(STEVE reaches over the side of the bed and picks up a pack of cigarettes. HE offers one to GRACE, SHE accepts, and THEY light their cigarettes from STEVE's lighter)

GRACE

(Blowing out smoke and touching him)

Steve . . . tell it to me again, darling.

STEVE

(Acting dumb)

Tell you what, baby?

GRACE

You know . . . what you used to tell me over and over when you first began seeing me.

STEVE

Oh . . . so, it's finally sunk in?

GRACE

Sorta . . . the words do seem to have more meaning.

(In happiness HE pulls her to him and kisses her)

STEVE

You're sweet . . .

GRACE

Awww . . . don't make fun of me . . .

(THEY break their embrace; STEVE holds her as HE speaks, an arm held loosely about her neck)

STEVE

Okay . . . listen closely . . . it's nothin' but meaning. It's by Kafka: "You do not need to leave your room. Remain sitting at your table and listen. Do not even listen, simply wait. Do not even wait, be quite still and solitary.

[41]

The world will freely offer itself to you to be unmasked, it has no choice, it will roll in ecstasy at your feet."

(A short silence; THEY draw upon their cigarettes, then speak)

GRACE

(Gushing)

Every time you repeat it, I get a little more out of it, you know what I mean, don't you?

STEVE

I think I do, Grace.

GRACE

Steve?

STEVE

Yeah . . . baby.

GRACE

What does that part mean?

STEVE

What part?

(GRACE turns away from him and sulks.

Leaning over her)

Awww, honey . . . what's wrong? What part are you talking about? You have to explain things . . . I don't know what you mean all the time.

GRACE

(Sullen)

Well, I've asked you before!

STEVE

Oh . . . that part . . . the part that says "The world
will freely offer itself to you to be unmasked . . ."?

GRACE

(Still facing away)

You know that's what I mean.

(HE *puts his arms about her and* SHE *relents a bit*)

STEVE

Haven't we talked about this before?

GRACE

Yes.

STEVE

And what have I said?

GRACE

(Bitter)

You've said "Because it has no choice . . ." But that's
not an answer, Steve. That's no answer!

STEVE

(Sincere)

But it is, darling. It is!

(Pulling her over)

It is! It really is, believe me! It is!

GRACE

(Reflective)

It . . . "will freely offer itself to you to be unmasked,
it has no choice . . ."

(Pause)

[43]

You know, you're so strange, Steve. Why do you work down at the plant?

STEVE

It's a job like any other, baby.

GRACE

For the other colored guys that . . .

STEVE

Honey, please . . .

GRACE

(Annoyed)

Oh, I forget! I forget you don't want me to say *colored* . . . that you want to be called at least *Negro* by stupid whites like me, or better, just plain *black,* or for the more *enlightened* . . . did you catch the pun, dear? . . . *Afro-American* . . . I forget! It's like I just said, somehow you came out different from those other Negroes or blacks or Afro-Americans down on the job . . . you're even different from the white guys . . .

STEVE

You better believe that!

GRACE

Awww . . . I don't mean it that way, honey. You just read more and study things that other guys don't know . . . and you're taking those night courses, not so you can get a better job, but so you can learn things other people don't know . . .

STEVE

(Correcting)

So I can learn what I don't know!

[44]

GRACE

You know I don't know how to express myself like I should
. . . Remember? I'm just a silly little secretary . . .

STEVE

Awww, c'mon, honey . . . lighten up.

GRACE

No! Why should I "c'mon and lighten up"? You walked
into the office one day for a time card and my world has
never been the same . . . with all your logic and ration-
ality . . . with all your white and black philosophy . . .
it's never been the same again, Steve. You just stand
around quiet and look out from behind those eyes all the
time. Never saying too much. Always treating me like
I'm something special when I know what you can do
with your mind. What are you waiting for? When the
manager is around your face is blank . . . you have
nothing to say but when we're alone you treat me like
a pet you're pampering . . . an animal you're fattening
up . . . for what, Steve?

STEVE

(Toneless)

See? You can express yourself when you want.

GRACE

Do you hate me so much?

STEVE

Hating is a foolish waste of emotional energies. Psychologically, it's defeating.

GRACE

See . . . you even forget to talk like a Negro sometimes when you're alone with me!

[45]

STEVE

How should Negroes talk, Grace?

GRACE

(Sorry)

Oh, you know what I meant, darling.

STEVE

How should we niggers speak to white folks, Miss Grace?

GRACE

I'm sorry, let's forget about it.

STEVE

How should we happy-go-lucky coons talk to you, Miss Ann?

GRACE

See, you do hate me!

STEVE

(Relieved)

Yeah . . . I guess I do, baby.

> (THEY *are separated, on opposite sides of the bed.* THEY *snuff out their cigarettes.* GRACE *reaches down and lifts a half-filled glass of juice and swallows the contents.* STEVE *fumbles with the radio dial and finds a rock 'n' roll station)*

GRACE

(Wistful)

Well . . . tomorrow is Monday . . . the Monday after our big holiday . . . and back to the grind, as the saying goes.

STEVE

(Pulling her close and attempting to kiss her)

Yeah, back to work. But it will be a lot different now.

GRACE

(SHE *turns partially and holds him)*

Different? Yes, I guess so . . . Steve, I want to talk to you about something.

STEVE

(Matter-of-factly)

What do you want to tell me, sugar?

GRACE

(Blithely)

Well, it's been a nice holiday . . . two weeks with nothing to do, just be together and take care of each other's needs . . . I really appreciate what you've done for me, I mean, you took my lonesomeness away . . . you've been so loving and thoughtful . . .

STEVE

What do you want to tell me, Grace?

GRACE

Oh, please, don't rush me, Steve. Let me talk to you.

(SHE *snuggles under him. Possessively,* HE *hugs her small waist. Her tears are on his shoulder)*

Steve, I've tried, I've tried. I've never had a man make me feel like you have . . . but it's only in bed that I feel anything for you . . . in bed! . . . after that . . . Oh, Steve, can't you understand?

STEVE

Understand?

GRACE

Yes, that we're from two different worlds . . .

STEVE

We're from many different worlds, aren't we? Yeah, I guess we are, aren't we?

GRACE

No, I don't mean that. I don't mean our colors . . . it's just that you see things different. Well, I just can't have the things I want if I keep loving you!

STEVE

The only thing I understand, Grace, is that you only allow yourself to believe what you think the world wants you to believe.

GRACE

Please don't argue with me . . . you know that I can't fight your arguments . . . but I know how I feel, Steve. I *know* how I feel.

STEVE

Why do you keep yourself tied up in knots; because of what? . . .

GRACE

(Cutting, shouting)

I don't! I don't! It's you!

STEVE

Shut up! I never played games with you. I told you from the first I loved you.

GRACE

Yes, you told me and I tried . . .

STEVE

I told you not to begin this thing with me if it wasn't going to last. Remember, remember what I told you? Remember the room I spoke of that you have shut against all the world?

GRACE

I won't allow you to keep turning everything into a dream, Steve. You live in some kind of fantasy world . . . we're no good for each other!

STEVE

(Continuing)

I asked you to allow me to enter your room, Grace, and you did.

GRACE

You're imagining things! I never allowed you anything. I refused you, Steve. But every time I said "no" was like a new battle you had to win. I've always refused you, Steve! I only have so much resistance.

(SHE *recoils from him)*

STEVE

At first. Only at first. These past two weeks I've been standing in the doorway to that room.

GRACE

You don't understand, darling. I only gave you my body, Steve. You have never had *me!* I've never been so happy in offering my body. Don't you understand?

STEVE

What do you want me to understand?

That you needed me. That I needed you. I gave my body to you and was happy that you were happy. Yes, I enjoyed it too . . . you give appetites to all the hungers of my flesh. I can't help myself when I'm making love with you. I love how you feel inside me . . . but it's not enough.

> (SHE *clutches him like* SHE *is about to sink below the surface of a pool)*

Please understand . . . it's not you, yourself, or anyone else but me. I've been with you these past two weeks constantly and we've been together occasionally over the last months. I've been made more happy than in years.

STEVE

Yeah . . . you've been happy, all right.

GRACE

Steve, I'm sorry I hurt you . . . I don't know what's wrong with me. I don't know what's wrong. For all I know, I may be carrying your child, but I still can't go on like this.

STEVE

Why?

GRACE

Because I can't, Steve.

STEVE

Why, Grace?

GRACE

I don't love you!

STEVE

Is that the real reason?

GRACE

(Bitter)

It's the only reason I know.

STEVE

Well, it doesn't matter.

GRACE

(On her elbows)

What do you mean?

STEVE

I told you not to begin this thing if you might do this to me.

GRACE

I know . . . I know, Steve . . . but I can't do anything about my feelings.

STEVE

You had feelings at the beginning . . . what happened to them?

GRACE

(Resigned)

I can't explain to you, can I?

STEVE

(Shouting)

Explain . . . explain?

GRACE

Steve . . . the neighbors!

STEVE

What is there to explain? What is there to understand?

[51]

I made my decision when I told you that I loved you.
You accepted that love.

GRACE

(Pleading)

I couldn't help myself.

STEVE

You entered into a contract . . . and you're going to
keep it!

GRACE

How can you talk about contracts now . . . your mind
is messed up from all those books by white men I know
that you hate!

STEVE

You don't know anything! There's things you don't understand, Grace. Man is the decider in this life. Man is
the creator of his situation, he, himself, is this.

GRACE

Please . . . don't . . . I'm tired . . . I don't want to
hear . . .

STEVE

My role, the role that I've made for myself, includes you
. . . we're inseparable . . .

GRACE

(Becoming scared)

We're not!

STEVE

The dream of myself isn't complete without you, darling.

[52]

GRACE

It is! It is, Steve. I'm no good for you! Get somebody else!
Get anybody! Get a black woman! Let her listen to all
that nonsense you learned out of those books!

STEVE

I didn't ask you if you were best for me; I decided that
and went after you with all I had. I made you see and
feel and want what you at first refused. I made you desire
me these past weeks.

GRACE

(Furious)

No! It was my own decision to spend these days with you
and it will be my decision when I end them.

(SHE *tries to pull away from him.*

HE *holds her under him)*

STEVE

I told you, Grace, not to come to me until you had fully
made your free choice . . . your free choice . . . nothing made you . . . remember, when it happens "it has
no choice" . . . no, not at all, baby. It was your choice
the moment you decided. And I'm holding you to it!

(SHE *jerks away and screams)*

GRACE

No! No! You're not! Not for me! I won't let you decide
anything for me!

(HE *grabs her shoulders and tries to hold her arms.*
SHE *sobs as* THEY *struggle)*

[53]

STEVE

(Whispering)

I'm not really deciding for you, darling, you made up your mind two weeks ago.

GRACE

(Jerking about)

Let go 'ah me! You let me go!!!

(SHE snatches one arm free and rakes his face with her nails)

STEVE

(Near hysteria)

You want to go back like nothin's happened? You want to go back like it was before . . . so you can treat me like a number . . . so you can look through me and around me and never see me . . . I love *myself* too much for that. You're mine and if you go back, you'll go back mine!

(His hands have moved to her throat. SHE scores a row of bloody welts down his chest. SHE gurgles until her wind is cut off. Her lips blue and eyes roll to the top of her head.

Finally, SHE relaxes with froth on her lips. SHE looks beautiful, her face blackened, near death.

STEVE jumps out of bed and dresses hurriedly. Picking up GRACE's panties from the dresser, HE dabs at the blood running down his face and chest. As HE fastens his last buttons GRACE regains consciousness and crawls to her knees. HE puts on his sport jacket and stands in the doorway, a book in his hand. Losing her grip on the bedboard, GRACE rolls from the bed to the floor, among the plates, ashtrays and other items, where SHE *gags and chokes.*

Standing over her)
Grace!

(SHE *looks up through tears)*

Same time tomorrow, okay?

(SHE *weakly nods yes and sniffles)*

(A bit louder)
Okay, Grace?

GRACE
(Nodding, sniffling; in croaking voice)
Okay, Steve . . .

STEVE
I think I'll enjoy making love to you tomorrow, darling.

(HE *turns and exits)*

BLACKNESS

THE HELPER

THE PEOPLE

THE HELPER
SISTER
MOTHER
BUDDY
DADDY

THE HELPER *was first performed at the New Dramatists'
workshop in New York City on June 1, 1970. Allie Woods
directed, and sets were designed by Richard Graziano.
Lighting was by David Bixler.*

The cast members and their roles are as follows:

THE HELPER	JAMES HAINESWORTH
SISTER	JUDITH DRAKE
MOTHER	MARTHA GREENHOUSE
BUDDY	RIK PIERCE
DADDY	JOSEPH HARDY

*Nonrealistic. Sets are painted white. But incautious
dashes of pastels suggest a banal attempt at differentia-
tion between the areas. The lights are glaring as if harsh
morning sunlight is streaming through curtainless panes.*

*Platforms on varying levels imply a very small one-
bedroom apartment. Each area has some identifying fur-*

niture or fixture: the kitchen has a stove, cabinet or chrome and plastic table; the bathroom has part of the toilet stool or tub showing; the living room has a couch and some chairs; the dining area, etc. A sense of limited space must be conveyed, even causing the actors to stumble over objects.

The lower levels suggest a hallway on the bottommost leading to the street and a stairway and various landings connecting the separate levels.

Upstairs, the platforms are crowded with boxes, filled to overflowing and tied. Chairs are stacked in corners, around tables and stands, and among piles of movables. A television chassis sits empty in one of the rooms, gaping and hollow, as the tube lies upon the floor, beside the shell, a squatting cyclops.

A calendar of a cowgirl, in only holsters and spurs, her crimson nails clashing with the flash of her silver pistols, takes aim, hanging from the wall above the television. This room is splashed with pink, with white baseboards slicing the pastel smudges of the walls into rough rectangular shapes.

The end of a scruffy white rug points out of the bathroom, rolled and tied by rope.

SISTER *sits upon the couch in the living room. Her sandy hair is tied by a bandanna and the blue Levis are faded dull.* SHE *wears an overlarge sweat shirt.* SHE *is a plump girl about twenty. Her actions are anxious.*

THE HELPER *enters from below and climbs the stairs, stands before the imaginary door to the apartment and checks an address on a small white sheet of paper.*

[57]

HE *pockets the note and knocks: knocking sounds from offstage as* SISTER *jumps slightly and bolts for the door.*

SISTER
(Opens door to a slit and peers through the crack)

You the helper?

(THE HELPER nods; SHE shuts the door, unfastens the night chain with a false clatter, snaps the lock back and pulls open the door for him to enter.

The sounds are heard clearly from offstage)

My husband ain't here now; he's gone to rent a trailer and car. My daddy and him will be back directly and they can help us.

(SHE leads him into the front room. Gestures toward couch)

Have a seat, won't you?

(HE sits. SHE sits in a chair across the room from him, out of the sunlight. THEY sit a minute, then SHE stands abruptly)

Would you like some coffee?

THE HELPER
Yes, black, please.

(Her chubby hands smooth down her sides, smoothing themselves against the bulges of her flesh. SHE walks into the kitchen)

SISTER
(From kitchen)

You sure you don't want anything in your coffee?

(THE HELPER doesn't answer. In his seat HE sits in the sunlight. HE wipes a sleeve across his brow and

[58]

moves his back against the pillows, scratching away
crawling sensations)

SISTER
(Returns with cup and saucer)

Here you go. You sure you don't want anything in it?

THE HELPER

No, thank you.

(SHE *returns to the kitchen and comes back shortly,*
clicking the cup upon her saucer. SHE *takes her*
seat once more and smiles. HE *sips his coffee, the*
steam and sun keeping his face moist)

SISTER   .

Are you in school?

THE HELPER

No, not now.

SISTER

Oh . . . I thought the employment office would send us
a college boy.

(THE HELPER *makes a loud noise sipping his coffee)*

We asked for a college boy who needed some extra work.

(SHE *quaffs her beverage down in deep gulps.*
Finally, SHE *stands looking warily at* THE HELPER)

We're going back up north. My husband and me . . .
we're going back to college in Oregon.

THE HELPER

That's nice.

(SHE *walks past the couch, her floppy shirt brushing*

past him, and peers out the window or its approximation, and looks each way up the street.

THE HELPER *lays his cup and saucer upon the floor and stands)*

SISTER
(Steps to center of the room)

You don't have ta . . .

THE HELPER
(Cutting, smiling)

That's okay. I'm a slow coffee drinker and I might as well begin.

(HE picks up one of the nearer cardboard boxes.

SHE scurries to the hall door, her tennis shoes squealing upon the bare floor)

SISTER
(Relieved)

Well, if you want to start now I don't see anything wrong with it.

(Opens door)

Here, let me show you where to put those things until my husband comes.

(Her topknot bobs and springs across the rag tying her head as SHE flounces down the stairs, leading THE HELPER to the entrance hall. Two wooden chairs set on each side of a table in the hall. Mirrors line the wall leading to the outside.

As THE HELPER lowers the box HE looks at his reflection in the mirror, watching the trail of sweat trickle to the end of his nose. From beyond his shoulder HE sees the girl's eyes in the glass)

SISTER

(Flustered as HE *turns)*

Well, I'll open this outside door and get things ready for
my dad and husband when they get here.

(SISTER *opens the imaginary door to the outside,
props it back with one of the chairs and goes off.
Upstairs,* THE HELPER *enters the apartment and
looks around. In a corner, beside a basket of news-
paper-wrapped dishes,* HE *pulls out an upturned
campaign sign, stick pointed at the ceiling, the
upside-down candidate smiling lipless out of a
dark blue background, his eyes bluer than the
background; all of the picture surrounded by a
red, white and blue starred border.*

THE HELPER *props the sign against the wall, lifts
a box and turns for his trip below, leaving the
poster grinning behind him.*

HE *makes repeated trips, gradually filling the downstairs hallway with boxes, occasionally receiving
aid from the girl who hurries in, rushes up the
stairs to inspect the progress and goes back usually
carrying two small items, such as glasses, plates or
lamps, in each hand.*

MOTHER *enters below and meets* THE HELPER *on
one of his trips)*

MOTHER

Ahhh . . . here's our little helper.

(MOTHER *is stout.* SHE *wears a crimson silk Chinese
coolie outfit; large brass bracelets swing from her
wrists, smaller loops pull her earlobes low; tied
about one puffed ankle is a golden chain with a
knotted heart, and grass thongs upon her feet make
shuffling sounds)*

[61]

(Entering)

This is my mother.

MOTHER

(Pointing)

Here, young man. You can put that box down there.

(SHE *steps out of his path. To his bending rear)*

That's darling of you.

SISTER

(To THE HELPER*)*

My husband and dad are out front hitching up the trailer.

(THE HELPER *nods and starts up the stairs)*

MOTHER

Sister, it looks like you've got a good start.

(Upstairs, THE HELPER *surveys what is left.* SISTER *goes off.*

MOTHER, *calling up the stairs)*

YOO HOO UP THERE! SOMEONE WILL BE UP TO GIVE YOU A HAND WITH THE REST OF THOSE THINGS.

(SHE *goes off.*

THE HELPER *drinks the remainder of his coffee.*

A gangling MAN *with glasses tilting on the edge of his nose enters below, wearing white coveralls with the insignia of an international airline, and climbs the stairs)*

BUDDY

(Looking through the rooms)

You've really got this place cleaned out.

(Lifting one end of a green table leaning against a wall)

Well, we might as well get the table-tennis equipment this trip.

(THEY *move cautiously downstairs, elaborately guiding the large table around the phantom stairwells.*

MOTHER *enters)*

MOTHER

Ohhh . . . be careful, fellows.

BUDDY

We will, Mother.

MOTHER

But *be* careful, Buddy. You remember the awful jar that boy gave the piano last summer in Waikiki.

BUDDY

Yes, I remember, Mother White.

(SHE *smiles at* THE HELPER *as* THEY *struggle around the last stairwell, and pats him on the shoulder when* HE *crosses the last step; her jewelry gives her a jangle)*

MOTHER

Oh, you both must be so tired to bring that thing down.

(SHE *peers at* THE HELPER's *face. To* THE HELPER)

Your sweating brings out such gorgeous tones in your

skin. I had this houseboy in Kingston . . . he was simply darling . . .

> (SHE *speaks to him as* HE *wrestles with his end of the bulky table)*

Buddy . . . take it right out to the trailer.

> (*With grunts the two* MEN *reach the bottom.* MOTHER *points, sweeping the swishing sleeves of her suit in a swirl toward the street)*

Take it right out to the street, Buddy.

BUDDY

Yes, that's where we're going.

> (SISTER *enters, followed by* DADDY)

SISTER

Ohhh . . . you guys are really coming along swell!

BUDDY

Won't ya please move out of the way, honey?

DADDY

What ya got there, Buddy?

BUDDY

The table-tennis table.

MOTHER

> (*To* DADDY)

Will we have room, Herbert?

> (SISTER, DADDY *and* MOTHER *block the hallway.* BUDDY *and* THE HELPER *drop the table and rest)*

DADDY

Of course we'll have room, Matilda.

SISTER

(Excited)

Mother, we got the biggest trailer made for cars . . . It's so big!

MOTHER

(Superiorly)

I know, dear . . . but is it big enough?

DADDY

Now, now, don't you worry none about that, Mother. We'll find a way.

BUDDY

But is it big enough, Mr. White?

SISTER

(Annoyed)

Of course it is, Buddy. Why . . . why . . . our trailer is painted orange and the very large twin doors in the rear are fastened back along the sides.

DADDY

(Informative)

It's big enough for chairs and hassocks and picture frames and everything.

MOTHER

(Making up her mind)

Well . . . I see it is a very American trailer . . .

SISTER

(Smugly)

Yes, it's hitched to a new Dodge.

[65]

DADDY

(To BUDDY*)*

Then you see, it'll do!

BUDDY

If you say so, Mr. White.

DADDY

(Hearty)

Here, Buddy, bring that table out here!

> (DADDY's *neck is freckled red and brown and his paunch is solid.* HE *is dressed in gray industrial trousers, green plaid woodsman shirt, and brown crepe-soled shoes.* HE *squints incessantly and there are the indentations of glasses straddling his nose.* SISTER *and* DADDY *lead the two carrying the table off.*)

> MOTHER *stands in the doorway, and when* THE HELPER *goes out* HE *steps upon her feet.* SHE *grimaces comically but in silence)*

DADDY

(Off)

Where are the net and paddles?

SISTER

(Off)

We put them in a box.

DADDY

Good . . . never know when you might need them.

SISTER

Slide it along the side, Buddy . . . Daddy . . . don't you think he should put it up against the side?

> *(Recovered,* MOTHER *gestures silently in the door-*

way and slightly pantomimes the action offstage through body English and feigning threatened disasters)

DADDY

(Off)

Yeah, slide it up that side next to them boxes, Buddy.

SISTER

Yeah, slide it up there, Buddy.

MOTHER

(From doorway)

Be careful sliding it like that . . . you know something dreadful *always* happens when we move.

DADDY

That's it . . . that's it . . . good boy.

(BUDDY and THE HELPER come in and climb the stairs. SISTER and DADDY come in and begin carrying the boxes stacked in the hallway outside. MOTHER follows the two young men.

SHE reaches the top as the two men begin lifting the fish tank)

MOTHER

Oh, the little precious babies . . . don't you dare frighten them.

(As BUDDY is taller, his end is higher than THE HELPER's. Sliding along the top of the glass, the water reaches the edge and spills a puddle over the side before THEY balance the container)

MOTHER

Ohhhh, dear, I told you. Oh, Buddy, please be careful

with the poor darlings. Remember, I got that aquarium in Hong Kong.

BUDDY

It's okay, Mother. We have everything under control.

MOTHER

I know that, dear boy. But be careful . . . will you?

(DADDY *looks up as the two creep down the stairs trying not to tip the tank*)

DADDY

Damn, where are we going to put that thing?

SISTER

We can't leave them, Dad.

DADDY

Yeah, yeah . . . I know.

(SISTER *and* DADDY *lead the two movers outside.* MOTHER *follows behind but doesn't leave the doorway*)

MOTHER

Now, put it some place where they'll be safe . . . understand? Safe!

DADDY

(Off)

Okay . . . okay . . . Matilda . . . just keep your pants on, will ya?

MOTHER

(Blustering)

Now don't you dare talk to me in that manner, Herbert White!

SISTER
Mother . . . Daddy . . . please . . . not here.

BUDDY
Wow . . . just feel this wind.

MOTHER
Ohhh . . . it's splashing the water.

DADDY
Yeah . . . it's fussin' with the skirts of these awnings like they were petticoats.

SISTER
Daddy!

MOTHER
Now watch your mouth, Herbert! Don't forget there are two white women in your presence.

DADDY
Shut up, Matilda! How in the hell could I ever forget you . . . even if you let me.

SISTER
Daddy!

DADDY
Buddy. Here . . . c'mon and put this thing in the car. Put it on the back seat there.

SISTER
But, Daddy.

BUDDY
I think it'll go.

DADDY
Sure it will.

MOTHER

Are you sure that's the correct place? Remember . . .

DADDY

PUT IT THE HELL IN THERE, BUDDY, AND LET'S GET THIS JOB FINISHED!

(MOTHER *stands exasperated with hands folded*)

SISTER

Put those boxes and bags and blankets around it.

BUDDY

Yeah . . . the cushions will protect it!

DADDY

Good . . . now let's have another look into that trailer.

BUDDY

Doesn't look so good, does it, Mr. White.

DADDY

We'll manage. Go on up and get the rest. Sister and me will move some of these things around.

(*The two young men climb the stairs to the apartment.* MOTHER *follows*)

MOTHER

(*To* THE HELPER *as* HE *lifts the bird cage*)

Now, take special care with Augustus' cage.

(THE HELPER *nods*)

Keep it covered. Don't let Augustus see your fingers or he'll bite. I warn you.

(THE HELPER *starts down*)

Buddy, that's right, take the dart board and the darts. . . . Do you want me to carry that bowling ball, dear?

[70]

BUDDY

No, Mother, it's not hard to carry with its special fabric carrying case.

MOTHER

Ohhh . . . good, boy . . . but it sure looks heavy.

(SISTER *and* DADDY *meet* THE HELPER *at the bottom of the stairs and call up to* BUDDY *too late, for* HE *has started down*)

SISTER

Come down here, Buddy!

DADDY

Now wait a minute, Sis.

SISTER

But, Daddy, we can't get any more in.

DADDY

Yes, we can, girl . . . we just have to try and push a little harder, that's all.

BUDDY

(Reaching bottom)

Let me help you, Dad.

(THEY *go off;* THE HELPER *goes up the stairs for another load*)

MOTHER

Herbert, if you shove that crate I got in Delhi down to . . . ohhh . . . he's gone.

(THE HELPER *comes down with a rubber plant. Looking up*)

You're going along marvelously, fellow.

SISTER

(*Distressed*)

Gee, I never knew we had so much . . . We're the Beverly Hillbillies . . . Jesus, we're the Beverly Hillbillies . . . the Beverly Hillbillies . . .

MOTHER

(*After* THE HELPER *passes*)

Sister, doesn't he have the most marvelous skin?

SISTER

(*Disinterested, starting up the stairs*)

Yeah, Mother . . .

MOTHER

So dark and rich . . . so . . . so African . . . Dear, let's go . . .

> (MOTHER *looks around and finds* SHE *is alone, so goes up the stairs after* SISTER.
>
> SISTER *is in the bathroom, having shut the imaginary door, and pulls down her pants and sits on the toilet seat.*
>
> MOTHER *enters the bathroom*)

SISTER

Mother, please.

MOTHER

Oh, stop complaining, dear. Remember, you're still my baby.

SISTER

(*Angry*)

Oh, Mother, please.

MOTHER

(*Continuing*)

It's just like yesterday when I was changing your diapers.
Now I'll be changing those of your children's soon . .
Sister? . . . You've been married two years . . . is there
anything wrong? I know that Buddy wasn't the best
choice you could make . . . your Daddy and I were very
against it, if you'll remember . . .

SISTER

(*Jumps up and pulls on her clothes*)

Oh, Mother . . . Oh, Mother . . . damn you!

(SHE *leaves.*

MOTHER *dabs water from the faucet on her hands
and follows*)

MOTHER

(*Cornering* BUDDY *at top of stairs*)

Now, after the card tables, dear, I want you to get the
rest of the potted plants . . .

BUDDY

Yes, Mother.

SISTER

(*To* THE HELPER *at the foot of the stairs*)

Now there's only the mattress and the bed springs left . .

(THE HELPER *nods*)

. . . and then the encyclopedias . . .

BUDDY

Yes, Mother.

[73]

. . . and the TV and chassis . . .

(THE HELPER *nods*)

MOTHER

. . . and the golf bags.

BUDDY

Yes, Mother White.

SISTER

. . . and don't forget the bathroom rug . . .

(THE HELPER *nods*)

. . . the clothes in the closets . . .

(HE *tries to get past*)

. . . and my bowling ball . . . My husband got his all ready.

(HE *starts up.*

DADDY *enters and follows them upstairs. The two young men begin carrying the last of the items down to the outside.*

DADDY, MOTHER *and* SISTER *stand about and supervise.*

Finally, DADDY *lifts the campaign poster and looks at it with worship, then reads the slogan*)

DADDY

(*Oratorically*)

IN YOUR SOUL YOU'RE SOLD ON HIM!

SISTER

(*Breathless*)

Amen!

[74]

MOTHER

What a wonderful man . . . how sad . . . how sad . . .

(THE HELPER *is busy finding a grip on the chassis.*

BUDDY *comes up and watches him*)

DADDY

(To BUDDY*)*

There won't be room for the chassis.

BUDDY

Oh, it don't matter anyhow, Dad. I got the set and can put it in any old chassis.

DADDY

Well, leave it down in the hall and me and Ma will come back this evening and take it over to our place.

(With a turn of his neck, the OLDER MAN *looks about the room once more, then walks to the cowgirl calendar and eases it off its nail and holds it in his hand, opposite the politician.*

Bowlegged, HE *goose steps from the room, down the stairs, holding the poster and calendar ahead of him like two banners.*

The movers continue their work.

BUDDY *and* THE HELPER *wrestle the box spring to the trailer*)

MOTHER

(To them)

You boys sure did a good job.

(THE HELPER *starts up again*)

BUDDY

We're leaving the frame and the mattresses . . . it's dirty.

[75]

MOTHER

But what will you sleep on, dear?

BUDDY

Oh, I guess we'll have to buy new ones, Mother White.

(*Upstairs,* THE HELPER *looks through the rooms and closets for anything forgotten.*

HE *finds* SISTER *in the bedroom changing her pants.*

HE *stands in the doorway watching her for a while, her back to him*)

THE HELPER

Is there anything else, Miss?

SISTER

(*Furious*)

WILL YOU PLEASE PARDON ME!

(HE *walks downstairs and finds* BUDDY *and the two older people in the hallway.* BUDDY *opens his wallet and pulls out several bills and hands them to* THE HELPER)

THE HELPER

Thanks.

(BUDDY *nods.* SISTER *comes downstairs.*

Before THE HELPER *turns to leave* HE *catches* DADDY's *stare for the first time*)

DADDY

(*Saluting*)

See you again, boy.

(THE HELPER *smiles, nods, pocketing his money, and exits*)

MOTHER

He sure was nice . . . I wish more of our help was like that.

SISTER

(Annoyed)

Mother!

BUDDY

Yeah . . . he was pretty helpful.

DADDY

(Looks balefully at his family)

Awww . . . if you kids want to think that . . .

(DADDY *spits on the floor*)

CURTAIN

A MINOR SCENE

THE PEOPLE

PETER BLACK
MISS ANN

A MINOR SCENE *was first performed at the Black Arts/West Repertory Theatre in San Francisco in Spring, 1966. It was directed by Hillery L. Broadous.*

The cast members and their roles are as follows:

PETER BLACK   HILLERY L. BROADOUS
MISS ANN   JUDY PERKINS

      MISS ANN *stands on a corner waiting for a bus.* PETER BLACK *strolls up, checks her out, and speaks:*

PETER

Hey, you white scummy-lookin' bourgeois bitch, take me to dinner?

ANN

Wha . . .

PETER

I said suck mah dick! In fact, suck outta mah ass!

[78]

ANN

Oh, dear . . .

PETER

You heard what I said, bitch . . . take me to dinner and suck mah dick and et cetera fa dessert.

ANN

Are you mad? I don't even know you!

PETER

Don't look at me out of your fuckin' ignorant, white face and ask stupid questions! You seen my pretty black face a hundred years sniffin' round your door for crusts of bread, pats on my woolly ass and fo sniffs out of ya asshole and armpits.

ANN

Stupid questions? Why should I take you to dinner, with your black face or not . . . and what has my white face to . . .

PETER

Fuck you . . .

ANN

Now listen . . .

PETER

Don't you want a new experience, Miss Ann?

ANN

Wha . . .

PETER

Do you just want to keep livin' in the same white rut all your life?

[79]

ANN

I think I'm going to call a cop.

PETER

You would, you white matha . . .

ANN

Don't you call me that.

PETER

Why shouldn't I? You stinkin' whoaah . . . That's what you are, aren't you? . . . A dirty, white . . .

ANN

No, you can't think that about me!

PETER

Why can't I, scumbag? . . . Huhhh . . . you'd call a cop . . .

ANN

No, you know I won't do that. I'm sorry.

PETER

Fuck you!

ANN

I'm sorry.

PETER

Kiss mah ass . . . you stupid complacent white skunk.

ANN

Please, I wouldn't call a policeman. I'm as scared of them as you are. You just upset me for a moment, that's all. I'm sorry.

PETER

Oh! When a nigger tells you he wants you to take him to

dinner you get upset and call the man, huh? When I tell you to suck mah dick you come up with your bullshit white liberal reasons why . . .

ANN

Don't say things like that! Don't call yourself a . . . well, just don't say that word, please.

PETER

What should I call myself, Miss Ann? What should I say to you white folks . . . yawhl? A Black man?

ANN

Please . . . don't say Black . . .

PETER

Fuck you!

ANN

I'm sorry.

PETER

Why shouldn't I say Black, you dumb spic 'n' span cunt? You're just like the rest . . . you're white . . .

ANN

Don't say that!!!

PETER

With your white man's blue eyes, and . . .

ANN

Oh, please, can't we go somewhere and eat? Where should we eat? I'm sorry.

PETER

Lookin' out of your white face . . . that skull you call a . . .

ANN

Do you like Chinese food?

PETER

Lookin' like your daddy round the nose and mouth . . .

ANN

Spanish? . . . Italian? . . .

PETER

Just a hollow shell of shit . . .

ANN

No, don't say these things!

PETER

A maggoty sack of fuckin' shit with skinny legs and a
flat butt . . .

ANN

Oh, please . . . let's go . . . let's go now, we can even
take a taxi.

PETER

Full of dead white pus . . .

ANN

I'm not like that!!! I didn't do it!!! I wasn't even there!!!

PETER

I shouldn't even let mah pretty self be seen with your
dead ass.

ANN

(Hails a cab)

Here's a cab . . .

(Holds out her hand)

Please, come with me . . . we can even get some of that
. . . what do you call it?

Soul food, bitch . . .

Yes, that . . . you'll come, huh?

Fuck you . . .

Ohhh . . . about that other thing . . . I don't think I
know how

Practice makes perfect.

Yes, it does. I'm sorry. I'm sorry. I'm sorry.

(His hand on her ass as THEY *wait for transpor*
tation)

Your place or mine, Miss Ann?

BLACKNESS

THE THEME IS BLACKNESS

*(A one-act play to be given before
predominantly white audiences)*

THE THEME IS BLACKNESS *was first performed in its original
form at various locations in the Bay Area—at San Francisco State College, at the Committee in North Beach,
during 1966–67. Following the basic dramatic structure
of the piece, music was later arranged and played by
Chebo Evans' Third World Three Black music trio. Also
Dewey Redman and Donald Garrett have contributed to
versions, with added sound effects by Black Arts/West.*

SPEAKER

The theme of our drama tonight will be Blackness. Within
Blackness One may discover all the self-illuminating uni-
verses in creation.

And now *BLACKNESS—*

> *(Lights go out for twenty minutes.
> Lights up)*

SPEAKER

Will blackness please step out and take a curtain call?

> *(Lights out)*

BLACKNESS

[84]

THE MAN WHO DUG FISH

THE PEOPLE

THE MAN: A tall, heavy Black man in his midforties. Impeccably dressed in the clothes of a financier. He has a fake Oxford or Cambridge accent, and carries an attaché case.

FISH STORE CLERK.

HARDWARE CLERK.

ASST. TO THE ASST. MANAGER OF THE BANK.

The FISH STORE CLERK, HARDWARE CLERK and ASST. TO THE ASST. MANAGER can be the same white actor, or Black actor in white mask or makeup.

THE MAN WHO DUG FISH *was originally published in* Nexus *(San Francisco: 1967). The play was first given a staged reading in the late '60's by the Theatre Company of Boston, then given a workshop production at The New Dramatists in New York City, June 1, 1970.*

Cast members for the later production are as follows:

THE MAN	FLOYD ENNIS
FISH STORE CLERK	HOWARD HONIG
HARDWARE CLERK	RIK PIERCE
ASST. TO THE ASST. MANAGER	BILL HARPER

Bare stage except for rough boards nailed together to make the counter.

Enter THE MAN *with briefcase.*

MAN

    (Clears throat)

Ahhh . . . heemmmm . . . this appears to be a hardware store.

    (Spot on the CLERK*)*

I say there, ole fellow.

CLERK

You mean me?

MAN

Yes, you . . . ahem . . . I mean I'd like some service.

CLERK

Well, why didn't you say it? What do you want? Our smelts are good today.

MAN

Smelts?

CLERK

Yes, smelts.

MAN

    (Incredulous)

In here . . . smelts?

CLERK

Yeah . . . and our perch ain't so bad either.

MAN
(Recovers)

Oh, smelts. Perch.

CLERK

And clams, lobsters, butterfish, porgies, oysters, scallops, crabs . . .

MAN

No. No. That won't do.

CLERK

Then sea bass, sturgeon, shad, shark, whitefish . . .

MAN

What do you have in a larger fish?

CLERK

Larger fish?

MAN
(Points)

Yes, like that fellow there.

CLERK

Oh, you want some trout?

MAN

Not exactly.

CLERK

But our trout are fine today.

MAN

No. No. I don't especially want trout.

[87]

CLERK

You don't?

MAN

No.

CLERK

No smelts 'cause they're too small . . . no trout 'cause you
don't 'specially want trout.

MAN

Yes.

CLERK

I see.

MAN

Really I mean no.

CLERK

No?

MAN

Yes, no smelts or trouts.

CLERK

Yeah, I'm sure I see what you're getting at.

MAN

You're so well informed.

CLERK

Well, I pride myself in my . . .

MAN

And so helpful.

CLERK

Now about our carp.

MAN

Carp?

CLERK

Yes, carp. Just what I think you need.

MAN

Carp?

CLERK

We got excellent carp today.

MAN

(Holds up attaché case)

You see . . .

CLERK

Yeah, a briefcase.

MAN

But . . .

CLERK

We get our carp fresh from the creek in back of here.

MAN

I want a fish . . .

CLERK

A little old lady catches it and sends it in to us . . .

MAN

. . . with head and tail . . .

CLERK

. . . by her grandson.

MAN

. . . a fish that will fit comfortably in this satchel.

[89]

CLERK

He rides a bicycle.

MAN

Can you find me a carp which will meet these requirements?

CLERK

English racing tires.

MAN

How nice.

CLERK

I'm here to sell fish, that's what I am.

MAN

(Beams and hands him attaché case)

Then put 'er there, my good man.

(Lights down. Lights up)

CLERK

And what size shovel would you like, sir?

MAN

Something not too big.

CLERK

Ahuh.

MAN

And not too small.

CLERK

Yes . . . yes.

MAN

Not too wide.

CLERK

I see.

MAN

Or not too slender . . .

CLERK

By all means.

MAN

. . . I don't want it mistaken for anything other than a
shovel . . .

CLERK

That is absolutely correct, sir.

(CLERK *pulls out a shovel*)

MAN

No.

(CLERK *pulls out another*)

No.

(CLERK *pulls out a third*)

Ah so!

(*Hands him the attaché case.*

Lights down. Lights up in the bank)

And what did you say the length was of this safety de-
posit box, Mr. Assistant to the Assistant Manager?

ASST. ASST.

Oh, this is our large standard size for your more heavy
valuables.

MAN

I see.

[91]

ASST. ASST.

Yes, everyone should have one.

MAN

Is that a fact?

ASST. ASST.

By all means, sir. They are moth proof, radar proof, fire-proof, earthquake proof, drop proof, heist proof, dirt proof, atomic-blast and dust proof, water free, airless, and they cannot be touched by another human hand besides yours . . . unless you die or we have a court order . . . naturally.

MAN

Naturally.

ASST. ASST.

(Hesitant)

Then . . . then . . .

MAN

I'll take it!

ASST. ASST.

Oh, goody.

MAN

And I'm paying ten years' rent on it.

ASST. ASST.

Ten years?

MAN

Yes, ten years. I'm about to take a long voyage.

ASST. ASST.

Long voyage?

MAN

Long.

ASST. ASST.

(Contemplating)

I see.

MAN

(Pulls bills from his wallet)

Will eleven hundred thirteen dollars and forty-one cents do?

ASST. ASST.

(Distracted)

Eleven hundred . . . oh, you mean you're paying with money?

MAN

Yes.

ASST. ASST.

That just can't be done, sir.

MAN

(Very British)

Nonsense!

ASST. ASST.

But just no one . . .

MAN

I insist!

ASST. ASST.

(Takes money)

Can you please wait a moment, sir? I must go speak to the Assistant to the Manager.

MAN

Very well.

> (ASST. ASST. *exits.* THE MAN *pulls the shovel from the briefcase and places it in the safe-deposit box, then pulls the still wet but very dead fish out, glowers at it, then places it in the box and locks it with the key.*
>
> *Enters* ASST. ASST. *as* THE MAN *pockets the key)*

ASST. ASST.

I'm sorry to have kept you waiting, sir.

MAN

And?

ASST. ASST.

(Quietly)

Just this once, sir.

(Secretive)

We'll relax our rules in your case . . . New customers are our privileged customers . . . ha ha . . . and all that rot . . . as you people say.

MAN

(Smiling)

Yes . . . and . . .

ASST. ASST.

You understand?

MAN

Surely.

ASST. ASST.

Is there anything you wish to place in your box at this time, sir?

MAN

No, nothing.

ASST. ASST.

(Lifts box)

Then I'll put it away.

(Knees nearly buckle)

My god, this seems so heavy! . . . Have you already used it, sir?

MAN

Not at all, my good man.

ASST. ASST.

(Tries to lift lid)

Would you mind . . .

MAN

(Wags finger)

Now . . . now . . . and you're the ones who make the rules.

ASST. ASST.

(Remorse)

Ohhh . . . sorry about that.

MAN

Perhaps you've put in a little too much time on this job, wouldn't you say?

ASST. ASST.

(Struggling off)

I guess you're right, sir. But . . .

(Hands box to THE MAN)

Feel how heavy it is.

Light as a feather.

(Pity)

My my . . . you do look peaked. Why don't you go get my receipt while I put this away?

ASST. ASST.

(Winded)

Excellent idea. But I believe I'll go home . . . get in bed, you know . . .

(Puffs)

. . . get a good rubdown by the Mrs. if she's home from her bridge club, or the country club, or the beautician's, or ladies aid society, or her women's club . . .

MAN

You need help, my dear man.

ASST. ASST.

Yes, yes . . . I'll have the Mrs. call the doctor as soon as I get home . . . if that's included in the budget this month.

MAN

(Good spirits)

Well, then cheerio, old sport.

ASST. ASST.

You'll lock up everything, won't you, sir?

MAN

Need you ask?

ASST. ASST.

It must be my head . . . or my liver or kidneys . . . or . . .

MAN

Or your heart . . . or your soul . . . my good man.

ASST. ASST.

(Sweating)

You can pick up your receipt on your way out.

MAN

Thank you, old chap. See you in ten years . . . and give my best to the Mrs.

(ASST. ASST. *exits as* THE MAN *begins tidying up and whistling "Columbia, the Gem of the Ocean")*

BLACKNESS

THE CORNER

The People

CLIFF DAWSON: Large, husky, a hint of a subdued swagger and worldliness about him. HE is light complexioned, brown, not yellow. Twenty-two years old.

BUMMIE: A bully but loyal. Medium height and athletic build. Nineteen years.

SLICK: Small, wiry and dark. Seventeen.

STELLA: Good figure on the heavy side. SHE wears her hair long and presses it daily with a hot comb, giving it a copper tone. Nineteen.

BLUE: Very dark with eyes and smile shining whitely from his face. Twenty-two.

SILLY WILLY CLARK: A progressive alcoholic who has never mentally grown older than sixteen. Brown-skinned, moon-faced, clothes always five years out of fashion. Twenty-four.

The people in this play are Black.

THE CORNER *was first performed at the Theatre Company of Boston in 1968. Direction by David Wheeler; set and lights by Robert Allen and Lance Crocker.*

The cast members and their roles are as follows:

SLICK	WILLIAM ADELL STEVENSON III
BUMMIE	GUSTAVE JOHNSON

STELLA	NOVELLA NELSON
BLUE	DICKIE EVANS
SILLY WILLY CLARK	DENNIS TATE
CLIFF DAWSON	JAMES SPRUILL

1. SPENDS IT ON ME

BUMMIE *and* SLICK *stand under the streetlamp on "the corner," passing a bottle of wine between them. It is the early '50's and* KING PLEASURE *sings "Moody's Mood for Love." Throughout the scene other music of the period plays.*

SLICK
(Drinks in gulps, takes a breath)
I sho feel sorry for you when Cliff gets here, Bummie.

BUMMIE
C'mon, man, pass the jug. Stella's gone into the store now.
'N that mathafukkin' cop might pass by any minute.

SLICK
We'll save Stella some . . . 'n mathafuk the cop! . . . 'N
his mamma too. I drink mah wine where I want to.

BUMMIE
You gonna save some for Cliff?

SLICK
Sheet . . . Cliff can get his own. We got this, didn't we?
And what chou worryin' 'bout Cliff for?

BUMMIE
I just got to look out for mah boy, Cliff, that's all.

SLICK
Like you looked out for his brother, Steve?

BUMMIE

(Drawing him out)

You mean you really ain't gonna save no wine for Cliff?

SLICK

Hell no! If you want him to have any then save him yours
. . . if I don't drink it up first.

BUMMIE

Man . . . you sho are cold.

SLICK

That's right . . . Hey, man, pass the bottle.

BUMMIE

I'm gonna tell him when he gets here. And laugh when
he kicks the cowboy shit out of you.

SLICK

He's gonna put his big foot up your ass before he does
mine.

BUMMIE

Nawh . . . I doubt that . . . I just fucked with his
brother . . . you're fuckin' with his wine.

SLICK

Shheeet . . . that big crazy mathafukker better not lay
his hands on me.

BUMMIE

He's not gonna lay his hands on you . . . he's gonna lay
his big foots on you . . . yeah, square in your ass.

SLICK

Hey, man, I thought you was my boy.

[100]

BUMMIE

I am. I'm your nigger if you gets no bigger . . . but I'm still gonna crack up seein' Cliff plant his big foots in your ass, man.

SLICK

Bummie . . . Bummie . . . you one of those humanitarian cocksuckers, man.

BUMMIE

What you call me, man? What kinda cocksucker is that?

SLICK

A humanitarian . . . you know . . . a do-gooder like . . . like Eleanor Roosevelt.

BUMMIE

Who?

SLICK

Roosevelt . . . Eleanor . . . well, look, man . . . You remember when you was a kid, don't cha?

BUMMIE

Yeah . . . but wha . . .

SLICK

And you us'ta go to the movies every Saturday . . .

BUMMIE

Yeah . . . man . . . we all us'ta go.

SLICK

Well, you remember when the news us'ta come on.

BUMMIE

Nawh, man . . . I don't know nothin' bout no news.

When that shit come on I'd have mah hand under some bitch's skirt or out gettin' some popcorn.

SLICK

But, man . . . you remember Eleanor Roosevelt . . . she was married to President Roosevelt.

BUMMIE

(Enlightened)

Oh . . . Oh! . . . Yeah . . . like that real black ole lady . . . Mary . . . Mary . . . what's-her-name . . . ya know, Mary somethin'-or-other.

SLICK

But she wasn't married to no president!

BUMMIE

Yeah, yeah . . . I know . . .

SLICK

Well, yeah . . . I know who you mean.

BUMMIE

Yeah . . . I know you do. *Her.*

SLICK

Yeah . . . like that broad who looks like your mama.

BUMMIE

Hey, man, I don't play that shit.

SLICK

Awww . . . man. You know I'm just jivin' . . . But she was at the White House and all that.

BUMMIE

I don't give a fuck where the old fat black bitch was . . .
I don't know nothin' about it.

(Pause)

Hey, man, what you mean I'm like her?

SLICK

I only said that you was kinda like a humanitarian . . .
and she and President Roosevelt's old lady and that white
cat out in the jungles wit' all them natives was the only
ones I thought about.

BUMMIE

Well, man, I don't want to hear nothin' bout some fat
ole-timey black bitch that I'm supposed to be like. Or
some ole white man runnin' 'round the jungles with a
bunch of savages.

(Takes SLICK's lapel)

I'm a man, and if you don't believe it I'll put my number
twelve up you for what you said I done to Steve.

SLICK

But, man, you shouldn'ta . . .

BUMMIE

Is dat any of your business?

SLICK

Awww . . . man, forget about it. Pass the bottle.

BUMMIE

Nawh.

SLICK

What you say?

BUMMIE

I said nawh.

SLICK

Hey, man, what's wrong with you? I went in on half for
that jug.

> (The confectionery store door opens and STELLA
> steps out)

BUMMIE

I don't care what you went in on, nigger. You ain't gettin'
no more. I'm savin' it for Cliff.

STELLA

Hey, give me a taste of your wine, Bummie.

SLICK

You just scared of Cliff . . . and want to kiss his ass because of Steve.

BUMMIE

Hi, Stell, how you doin', baby?

> (HE *hugs her waist*)

STELLA

Give me some of that wine, Bummie.

SLICK

You a chickenshit mathafukker, Bummie.

BUMMIE

If I didn't have hold of this girl I'd kick your ass, smart
nigger.

SLICK

> (*Furious*)

You would! You would!

BUMMIE

(Holds bottle in front of STELLA*)*

You want some of this stuff, baby?

STELLA

You know I do, man. You gonna keep it all for yourself?

BUMMIE

Nawh . . . baby. Here . . .

(Hands her the bottle)

SLICK

Hey, Bummie, man, what about me?

BUMMIE

You had yours, smart mouth.

SLICK

(Whines)

Awww, man . . . I paid for that wine just like you and look at it. . . . The way Stella swills it won't be any left.

STELLA

(Takes breath)

What you mean I swill?

*(*SHE *takes another swallow)*

SLICK

Ahhh, baby . . . not so fast.

*(*SHE *gives bottle to* BUMMIE*)*

STELLA

That sure was good. Thanks.

[105]

BUMMIE
(Kisses her cheek and pats her rear)

That's okay, baby. Anytime.

STELLA
(Pulls away)

Go on, man . . . with that stuff.

SLICK

You gonna save the rest for Cliff, Bummie?

BUMMIE

Nawh.

SLICK

You gonna give me the rest?

BUMMIE

Nawh.

SLICK

You gonna drink it all up by yourself?

BUMMIE

Nawh.

STELLA

What you gonna do with it, Bummie?

BUMMIE
(Pulls STELLA *in by her waist)*

Me and you's gonna drink it, Stella.

STELLA
(Teases SLICK*)*

That's really nice of you, Bummie. Really it is.

SLICK

I put my money into it . . .

BUMMIE

(Drinks)

Relax.

(Pause)

Cliff'll get a jug when he gets here . . . always does.

STELLA

Ha ha . . . all Cliff is gonna get is a piece of your butt
Bummie.

BUMMIE

Hey . . . baby . . . why you got to sound on me like
that?

SLICK

But he might not can get any money off'a his ole lady.

STELLA

Because I dig you, honey.

SLICK

(Whines)

But he might not can get any money off'a his ole lady.

STELLA

Who? That little broad of his named Lou? She'd give him
her last quarter . . . silly as she is.

SLICK

She might not have it . . . and I paid my money for
that jug.

BUMMIE

Shut up, lil chump! You need to be learned a lesson.

STELLA

You teachin' Slick a lesson, Bummie? You always teachin'
somebody somethin', man.

SLICK

Teachin' somethin' when he don't know shit.

BUMMIE

(To STELLA)

Yeah, baby. The lil young blood's gettin' out of hand . . .
thinks he's bad or somethin' . . . like Steve . . .

(Ironic)

Got to show him his place, ya know?

STELLA

(Teases)

Yeah, I know how it is with these youngsters. Don't even
have any respect anymore. Pass the bottle, won't cha, hon?

BUMMIE

Sho, baby.

(Hands her the bottle)

SLICK

Awww . . . you shouldn't do nothin' like that.

STELLA

(Breath)

These hare young blood's bones ain't hard enough . . .
right, Bummie?

BUMMIE

You said it, Stell. Little jive suckers . . . don't even know
how to talk when they around ya.

SLICK

(Angry)

I hope Cliff don't come. I hope Lil don't give him no fucken money to spend on you.

STELLA

(Breath)

He'll come. He knows I'm here.

SLICK

You here? Sheeet . . . woman, he don't care if you here or on the moon.

STELLA

(Drains bottle)

Yes, he does. He's only with that little bitch cause she works and gives him money. But he spends it on me.

SLICK

(Coldly furious)

Spends it on you? You mean he buys you a bottle of wine to drink with him before he screws you?

(Mocking)

Spends it on you? . . . He don't even buy you a hotel room at night . . . ha ha ha . . . Spends it on you? . . . How many times you've spent in the back seat of Silly Willy's broke-down Buick that don't run no mo'?

(Names her)

Spends it on you . . . you weak-minded bitch! How many times you been on *my* couch . . . in *my* front room . . . with him?

(Cruel)

Spends it on you . . . Ha ha ha . . .

(To BUMMIE*)*

Man . . . I can hear those old springs just'a squeakin'
. . . "Squeak'a . . . squeak'a .. . squeak'a" . . . Spends
it on you. I can hear Stell here sayin' from through the
wall in the other room: "Don't you love me, Cliff, baby?
. . . Don't you care 'bout me some, Cliff, huh? . . .
ha ha . . . Spends it on you?

(SHE *throws the empty wine bottle at* SLICK; *it
misses*)

STELLA

Punk! Faggot!

SLICK

Hey, woman, stop that!

(*Wry*)

You could hurt me and my pretty self.

BUMMIE

(*Laughing*)

Hey, man . . . lighten up on the pore broad.

(STELLA *tries to scratch* SLICK's *face*; HE *holds her
arms*)

SLICK

Hey, Bummie, help me. Help me, man, get this crazy
bitch off'a me.

BUMMIE

I ain't in it. . . . Ha ha ha . . . I ain't in it. I hope she
kicks your little ass.

SLICK

(*Breathing hard*)

Stella . . . you better stop foolin' round or I'm gonna
knock you on your big ass.

(*Angry*)

You just do it, mathafukker! . . . You just do it.

(SILLY WILLY CLARK *and* BLUE *turn the corner and enter the light.* THEY *are drunk*)

BLUE

Hey . . . mathafukkers . . . what's happenin'?

SILLY WILLY

(*Stumbles, giggles*)

What you doin't to that girl . . . lil Slick nigger?

SLICK

(*Still holding her*)

I ain't doin' nothin', man . . . Hey, Blue . . . Hey, Silly Willy . . . get this simple bitch off a me.

SILLY WILLY

Awww . . . you simple niggers . . . Later for all that shit . . . have a drink.

(HE *takes a bottle from his back pocket and lifts it*)

BUMMIE

A drink?

BLUE

Yeah, man, a drink.

(STELLA *quits her wrestling*)

STELLA

I'm gonna git you, Slick.

SLICK

(*Pats her butt as* THEY *break*)

Awww˙ . . Stell . . . you knows I loves you.

[111]

STELLA

Fuck you, punk!

BLUE

Oooeee, Slick . . . you gonna take that shit?

BUMMIE

You ain't signifyin' . . . is you Blue-Black, friend of mine.

(THEY *gather in a circle under the street lamp and
pass the bottle around*)

BUMMIE

Old Silly Willy Clark . . . I knew you were good for
somethin' . . . You fat-head mathafukker.

SILLY WILLY

But you ain't gonna be when Cliff catches up with you.

BUMMIE

(Apprehensive)

He's lookin' for me?

SILLY WILLY

(Shrugs)

Uummmmmmm ummm . . . is he?

SLICK

What you go and punch his brother for and pull a thirty-
eight on him when he tried to fight back?

BLUE

You know how Cliff feels about his little brother.

STELLA

Is Cliff gonna get you, Bummie, huh?

[112]

(Scared)

Nawh, woman.

(Boasting)

Ain't nobody gonna get me.

SLICK

If Cliff don't . . . Steve will. That's an evil little nigger.

BLUE

Yeah . . . that little nigger's mean . . . He'll sneak you if he can't get you any other way.

BUMMIE

Awww . . . why don't you people quit fuckin' with me?

BLUE

Hey, I got one . . .

(Pulls out another bottle)

STELLA

Let me drink out of yours, Blue, honey.

BLUE

Sho, baby.

STELLA

Silly Willy probably slobbers in his.

SILLY WILLY

Slobbers!

STELLA

I can't even kid with you, can I, sweetie pie?

SLICK

You better stop flirtin' wit' the fellas, Stella.

STELLA

You mind your business, man. Everybody knows I'm Cliff's girl.

SLICK

Then stop messin' wit' the fellas . . . you just gave ole Silly here a hard-on.

(BLUE *and* BUMMIE *laugh.* SILLY WILLY *half-turns, half-crouches, hand over groin, and takes another drink*)

2. THE CORNER

Time passes.

The Corner. BLUE, STELLA, SILLY WILLY *and* BUMMIE *drink.*

BLUE

You can drink out of my bottle anytime you wants, Stella.

STELLA

(Tipsy)

Thanks, baby.

SILLY WILLY

Where's Cliff Dawson?

BUMMIE

He ain't come up yet.

BLUE

I better save him some.

STELLA

(Tilts head back and takes a long drink)

Yeah . . . you do that.

BUMMIE

Wow . . . this broad sho can put it away.

SLICK

Well there's the sharks . . . and there's the fishes.

BLUE

Some fish are called suckers, man. You hip ta that?

SILLY WILLY
(To STELLA, *still drinking)*

Kill it, girl!

(Hysterically)

Heeeee ha ha ha . . . let me see how ya do it!

3. THE TAKING

Later.

"The Corner." CLIFF *and* STELLA *stand under the street lamp.*

CLIFF

You niggers drank up everything, huh?

STELLA
(Drunk)

I tole them . . . I tole 'em . . . I tole 'em not to . . .

CLIFF

Well, I don't give a fuck, see?

STELLA

. . . do it. Tole 'em not to do it or . . .

CLIFF

I can get a drink whenever I want.

[115]

STELLA

They over to Slick's, baby. They over there, Cliff.

CLIFF

Was it that little Slick nigger who drank up everything?

STELLA

Yeah . . . yeah . . . it was him. It was Slick. I tried to
save you some but . . . hey, ain't you goin' over to Slick's,
Cliff?

CLIFF

Nawh, I ain't goin' over there.

STELLA

You're not? . . . Awww, Cliff. They probably got another
Big Man 'a wine and just waitin' for you. C'mon, Cliff.
Let's go. Please?

CLIFF

Nawh . . . let 'em keep it. And what the fuck you want
some more to drink for? Ya can hardly stand now. C'mon
. . . let's go.

STELLA

Where, Cliff?

CLIFF

C'mon, let's go sit in Silly Willy's car.

STELLA

Nawh, Cliff. Nawh . . . I don't want to do nothin' in
there no mo.

CLIFF

(Jerks her)

C'mon, woman . . . let's go!

[116]

STELLA

(Whines)

Awww . . . Cliff . . . nawh . . . I don't want to go.

CLIFF

What do ya mean ya don't want to go?

STELLA

(Drunk)

I'm not a tramp, Cliff . . . Ah'm not a tramp.

CLIFF

Don't argue with me, bitch! When I say come . . . I mean just that!

STELLA

Don't do this to me, Cliff.

CLIFF

(Pulls her)

Come on!

STELLA

Don't, Cliff!

CLIFF

Now what you actin' like a fool for?

STELLA

You can take me somewheres besides that ole car. You can take me somewheres.

CLIFF

C'mon, we just gonna sit and talk.

STELLA

Oh, stop lyin', man. You know I want you, baby. But not

[117]

in no back seat of some fuckin' broke-down car all the time.

CLIFF

(Pushes her)

Shut up!

STELLA

Take me to a motel, Cliff.

CLIFF

What?

STELLA

Please . . . Cliff . . . please. Take me to a motel, Cliff . . . just once.

CLIFF

What's wrong with you, woman?

STELLA

Just this once, Cliff. Just this once.

CLIFF

I ain't got no money to be wastin' on that foolishness, woman!

STELLA

Yes, you have, Cliff. I know you have money . . . I know it! You keep money . . . you get it from that girl you live with . . . Lou.

CLIFF

It ain't none of your business what I get, bitch! You don't know nothin' bout mah business. You just keep your mouth shut, ya hear?

Nawh, I ain't gonna keep mah mouf shut! I ain't no whore, Cliff. I'm a woman . . . I want to be your woman. I don't care none about Lou or Sue or Annie or any of the rest of your funky bitches . . . just as long as you treat me right. But this ain't right, man. This ain't right.

CLIFF

It ain't? It ain't right?

STELLA

Nawh, it ain't right, Cliff. I do anything for you . . . you know that. I do almost anything 'cept get out on these streets for you.

CLIFF

You gonna do that before it's all over with.

STELLA

Don't say that, Cliff. You don't mean that, do you? You wouldn't have me do that, would you? You don't have that bitch Lou on the street. She ain't on the block!

CLIFF

Nawh, because she's in the laundry. In the laundry bringin' home that paycheck every week.

STELLA

(Crying)

And you want me to go out on the street.

CLIFF

You out here all ready. All you got to do is make it pay.

STELLA

You sonna bitch . . . you know I ain't doin' nothin' like that!

[119]

CLIFF

C'mon, baby . . . let's go to the car.

STELLA

Ohhh . . . Cliff . . . please. Please, Cliff.

CLIFF

Let's go to the car, Stell.

STELLA

Tell me I don't have to go out on the block, Cliff. Tell me that.

CLIFF

Let's go to the car, Stell.

STELLA

Let me talk to you, baby.

CLIFF

The car.

STELLA

Please . . .

> (THEY *start off and* CLIFF *kisses her;* SHE *clutches him and* HE *pulls away and* SHE *stumbles after him into the shadows)*

STELLA
(From the shadows)

I'm yours, baby . . . but don't treat me so bad. Just don't treat me so bad.

4. IT'S TOO LATE NOW

Two hours after.

The Corner.

CLIFF, BUMMIE, SLICK, BLUE *and* SILLY WILLY CLARK *stand under street lamp.* ALL *are drunk except* CLIFF.

CLIFF
What a motley-ass bunch of cheap mathafukkers!

BUMMIE
We sorry, man. I tried to get them . . .

CLIFF
Awww . . . shut up! I'm through with you all. All of you.

SLICK
Cliff . . . don't be like that.

(CLIFF *slaps* SLICK)

CLIFF
You . . . little nigger . . . I heard about you.

BLUE
Hey, Cliff . . . cool it.

SILLY WILLY
Everythin's gonna be all right, Cliff. C'mon, let's go up on the avenue.

SLICK
Man . . . you shouldn't ah done that. It wasn't just me.

CLIFF
Nawh . . . I ain't goin' nowhere. I'm through with you niggers.

BUMMIE
Ahhh . . . Cliff . . . we sorry.

BLUE

Forget it, man.

CLIFF

Nawh, I ain't gonna forget nothin'. I'm sick of you all
. . . all of you. Just came from down the street in that
broke-down car with Stella. Bitch so damn drunk she fell
asleep on me . . .

(Offers car key)

Here . . . here's the car key . . . you niggers can go
down there and wake her up if you can.

BUMMIE

(Incredulous)

Man . . . you don't care . . .

BLUE

Do you know what you sayin', Cliff?

SILLY WILLY

Give me that goddamn key. I always did want some of
Stella . . . good as she looks.

(SILLY WILLY *takes key)*

SLICK

Cliff . . . you ain't gonna be mad tomorrow, are ya?

CLIFF

Do you think I'm gonna be mad? What makes you think
I care what you niggers do?

SILLY WILLY

C'mon . . . let's go.

BUMMIE

Hey, you guys . . . I'm not goin' . . . I'm not gonna do
nothin' like that.

BLUE

But, man, if Cliff don't care . . .

SLICK

Now, Cliff . . . Cliff . . . if we do you ain't gonna be mad, are ya? If you get mad at one of us, man . . . you got to get mad at us all.

CLIFF

Go on, man . . . enjoy yourself. She's yours. All of you deserve each other.

SILLY WILLY

(Starts off)

I knew I had a good reason for buyin' that car.

BLUE

(Following)

Shssss . . . man. Somebody might hear us.

SLICK

Look, man . . . I'll get a jug tomorrow, hear? I'll bring it by your house.

SILLY WILLY

(Singing)

Stella . . . Stella . . . our little fancy bella . . . we're comin' ta be your fellas.

CLIFF

Get the fuck out of my face . . . little Slick nigger.

BLUE

(From shadows)

Shsss . . . quiet, man! Stop dat singin', Silly, man.

(SLICK exits.

Silence. CLIFF and BUMMIE stand on the corner)

BUMMIE

What's wrong, man? Huh? What's wrong?

CLIFF

You don't know?

(Silence)

BUMMIE

Well . . . man . . . you know Steve don't like me none.

CLIFF

But you sneaked him, Bummie.

BUMMIE

But he was gonna do the same thing to me, man. I could
see it comin', man.

CLIFF

You could see it comin', huh?

BUMMIE

Yeah . . . Cliff. I could.

(Pause)

CLIFF

Well . . . that's between you and him. Steve can take
care of himself.

BUMMIE

(Relieved)

Well, thanks, man . . . I'm sorry about . . .

CLIFF

But you know he's not gonna forget it, Bummie. He's that
way, man.

BUMMIE

Yeah, I know.

CLIFF

I'll talk to him. He's always listened to me.

BUMMIE

Cliff . . . is there anything really bothering you, man?
You don't . . .

CLIFF

(Annoyed)

Awwww . . . man . . . it's just one of those goddamn
days, I guess.

BUMMIE

But somethin' had to happen, man. This ain't like you,
Cliff.

CLIFF

What's like me, huh? To be a bum? To drink wine and
fuck bitches in junky cars? To stand half the night on
some street corner that any fucken cop can come up and
claim? . . . Is that like me?

BUMMIE

But, man, we've always done it. Even before you went
into the Navy and got out.

CLIFF

But I ain't doin' it no more, Bummie . . . no more.

BUMMIE

Are you goin' away, man?

CLIFF

Nawh . . . nawh . . . not goin' away no more. Not anymore . . . I'll be here for a long time, man. I'm a family
man now.

BUMMIE

You and Lou are gonna get hitched?

CLIFF

Hitched? Hummp . . . that's funny . . . I never thought about that.

BUMMIE

You gonna settle down, man?

CLIFF

Yeah, Bummie, yeah. Lou's gonna have a baby. I'm gonna be a father.

BUMMIE

Well . . . I'll be damned.

CLIFF

Yeah . . . you can start callin' me Daddy Cliff.

BUMMIE

Hey . . . man . . . that's great. C'mon up on "the avenue" . . . I'll buy ya a drink.

CLIFF

Nawh, man. I'm not up to it. I'm goin' in.

BUMMIE

Hey, man, you changin' already.

CLIFF

Yeah, maybe I am. Well, I'll see ya, man.

(CLIFF *exits.*

BUMMIE *stands a moment whistling, shuffling his feet with hands in his pockets and then exits in the direction of* SILLY WILLY's *car)*

BLACKNESS

II Introduction:

THE BLACK REVOLUTIONARY COMMERCIAL

In San Francisco, during the Spring of 1967, LeRoi Jones (traditional name: Imamu Amiri Baraka) worked with Black Arts/West, The Black House, and The Black Students' Union of San Francisco State College through a Black Arts coalition called The Black Arts Alliance to implement a Black Communications Project.

One of the numerous activities of the writers of The Black Arts Alliance was the writing of Black Commercials for use as short, low-budget films that could be distributed nationally—quickly and economically—throughout Black communities.

We knew that the major means of communication to Black people in America is television. Then film. And we realized that the technical form of the television commercial was recognized by this Black audience on a mass subliminal basis and that we could utilize the forms but change the content, thus producing a revolutionary mass communications tool.

A number of Black Commercials were written by LeRoi Jones, Marvin X and myself. All of mine were destroyed except the following (*Black Commercial #2*) during a period of imprisonment when the San Francisco police harassed The Black House, our headquarters with Eldridge Cleaver, and The Black Panther Party for Self-Defense. Marvin X and I were arrested and held in various jails in the Bay Area until The Black Arts Alliance freed us.

Soon afterward The Black House disintegrated and The Black Arts Alliance concentrated on creating a documentary film *(Black Spring)* and doing plays throughout California.

ED BULLINS

February 26, 1969
Harlem

BLACK COMMERCIAL #2

FADE IN:

Scene: Saturday night. "The Place," a pig-feet emporium and whiskey, beer, and wine joint in the Black community. Black people so close that the air can be sliced in squares, packaged, and shipped north, as "soul."

The CROWD *watches* RUFUS *and* BLUE *as they occupy the dance floor.* RUFUS *and* BLUE *are killing each other.* RUFUS *has a broken beer bottle and is trying to gouge* BLUE'S *eyes out.* BLUE *holds his friend's arm with one hand and is kept from driving his bone-handled switchblade into* RUFUS *by the man's tenacity to remain alive.*

RUFUS
(Huffing)
Ya black mathafukker . . . I'm gonna kill ya.

BLUE
(Puffing)
Kiss ma ass ya jive mathafukker! . . . I'm . . .

CROWD *(the Black Chorus)*
KILL KILL KILL . . . THAT BLACK MATHAFUK-
KER!

RUFUS
I'm gonna cut ya up and down.

[131]

BLUE

Ah'm gonna cut ya side ta side.

CROWD

KILL KILL . . . CUT 'EM UP 'N DOWN . . . SIDE
TA SIDE . . . 'N 'CROSS DE CROSS . . . KILL!
KILL!

RUFUS

Ah'm gonna fuck ya up so bad ya mamma won't have ya.

BLUE

Black mathafukker! . . . I don't play that shit . . . just
you wait!

(THEY *tussle more furiously*)

CROWD

BLOOD! BLOOD! BLACK BLOOD! BLACK BLOOD!

RUFUS

Let me go, nigger . . . so I can kill ya!

BLUE

Nigger . . . just you wait until I git mah knife in ya ass!

(A *young* BLACK MAN *steps out of the* CROWD. *He
is neatly dressed and speaks softly*)

BLACK MAN

Brothers.

(The TWO *stop fighting*)

RUFUS

What you say, man?

BLACK MAN

Brothers.

RUFUS/BLUE

(Together)

Huh????

BLACK MAN

Brothers.

BLUE

You mean you think him and me is brothers?

BLACK MAN

Brothers.

CROWD

(Intermittent voices, bewildered)

BROTHERS! BROTHERS! BROTHERS! BROTHERS!
BROTHERS! BROTHERS! BROTHERS! BROTHERS!
BROTHERS!

(Grows more confident)

BROTHERS   BROTHERS   BROTHERS   BROTHERS
BROTHERS   BROTHERS   BROTHERS   BROTHERS
BROTHERS   BROTHERS   BROTHERS . . .

RUFUS *(to BLUE)*

If we brothers, man . . .

BLUE

(Perceiving)

Yeah . . . then . . .

RUFUS

(Recognizing)

Why . . . brother . . .

(RUFUS *helps* BLUE *up.* BLUE *begins brushing his brother off)*

[133]

Black.

(Chants)

Black brothers Black brothers Black brothers . . . Black Black . . .

> (BLACK MAN *steps back into the* CROWD *and becomes one of them as* RUFUS *and* BLUE *clasp hands and speak of their mutual plans for the future, working in unity)*

Salaam . . . Salaam . . . Salaam . . . All Praises Due to the Black man, etc. . . .

FADE OUT:

THIS BLACK PUBLIC AFFAIRS ANNOUNCEMENT WAS MADE POSSIBLE THROUGH YOUR NATIONAL BLACK CONSCIOUSNESS BROADCASTING COMPANY (BCBC).

> April 12, 1967
> The Black House
> San Francisco

THE AMERICAN FLAG RITUAL

(*A Short Play or Film Scenario*)

FADE IN:

A young Black man.

He enters. Under his arm is a bulky object. Tied by cord.

The man kneels and unties the bundle. Carefully, he winds the cord into a ball and deposits it into his pocket.

After he pulls his hand from his pocket, he stands, looks down at the unwrapped bundle, then kneels again.

He slowly unfolds a large American flag.

Faint music in the background—music to suggest a solemn, ceremonious, religious, official public act is to be performed.

The flag is unfolded. The man stands in its center, just a bit southeast of the field of blue and the white stars.

He reaches into his pants fly, pulls his penis from his pants, and upon the initial tones of the American National Anthem, begins to urinate on "Old Glory."

As he relieves himself, the music plays and finally dies down and stops as his last drops dribble to an end. . . .

He shakes himself, puts his joint away, zips his pants up, wipes his feet on the "Stars and Stripes," then exits.

May 21, 1969
Harlem

STATE OFFICE BLDG. CURSE

(*A Scenario to Ultimate Action*)

Site of the New York State Office Building at 125th Street and 7th Avenue in Harlem.

First day of public opening—OPEN HOUSE.

Out front, on the sidewalks: politicians, American flags, Harlem crowds, Black National flags, numerous cops and plainclothesmen.

Speechmaking by Rockefeller, Lindsay, Javits, Chisholm, Rangel and Sutton. Maybe Powell.

Ribbon cutting. Crowds pour into building for look/see. Black crowds to see the false marble madness. Brothers in Afros and clean heads and just heads. Sisters with the brothers. Children. Some older Black people unattached to the artificial integration political machine.

Black folks checking out the cement tomb, Black folks on pig-guided tours, wandering alone around the tunnels and caves of the Twentieth Century crypt, examining the files, getting lost in the basement, in the rest rooms.

Closing. All out. Black people ushered out by guards and cops. American flags lowered as night sets on Harlem.

Later: hours later. Way into the black night. Exterior of the State Office Building. Quiet 7th Avenue at that hour. Almost deserted 125th Street at 3 A.M.

Explosion rips the whole State Office Building apart. Fire. Torn out windows. Total destruction through explosives.

Fire engines. Police. Harlem crowds. TV camera men. Photographers. Silent brothers and sisters standing on far side of the street looking knowingly at each other.

And the Black crowd senses the moment in Revolutionary Black History and begins a festival to celebrate the emerging Black nation of Harlem.

BLACKNESS

November 12, 1969
Harlem

ONE-MINUTE COMMERCIAL

(For Black Community Broadcasting)

(MAN's *footfalls on floorboards*)

WOMAN'S VOICE

Play E-5, baby.

(*Sound of coin going into record player slot, the coin falling and rattling, activating the machine.*

E-5 *comes on*)

1ST MAN'S VOICE

You're from The New Lafayette Theatre, ain't chou, man?

2ND MAN'S VOICE

Yeah, my brother.

1ST MAN'S VOICE

What'cha doin' now, man?

2ND MAN'S VOICE

We open A Ritual to Raise the Dead and Foretell the Future on Friday, February sixth, my brother.

1ST MAN'S VOICE

No jive?

2ND MAN'S VOICE

No jive.

1ST MAN'S VOICE

On February sixth?

2ND MAN'S VOICE

Yeah, Friday, February sixth, by the Western calendar,
my brother, but the year 6000, in the month of . . . well
let's wait until the day you come . . . but that day will
be a day on the Blackness calendar.

1ST MAN'S VOICE

Square business?

2ND MAN'S VOICE

Square business.

1ST MAN'S VOICE

The New Lafayette Theatre?

2ND MAN'S VOICE

Yeah . . . The New Lafayette Theatre at 137th St. and
Seventh Ave. in Harlem.

1ST MAN'S VOICE

(Slowly)

To Raise the Dead and Foretell the Future.

2ND MAN'S VOICE

At 137th Street and Seventh Ave. in Harlem.

1ST MAN'S VOICE

The New Lafayette Theatre.

2ND MAN'S VOICE

Yeah . . . you got it. . . . Well . . . later . . .

1ST MAN'S VOICE

Say, brother?

Yes, my brother?

You gonna shave your head again this time?

Hey . . . hit F-8 fo' me, honey!

END

December 26, 1969
Harlem

A STREET PLAY

Harlem. 125th Street. On one of the corners.

ACTOR 1 *walks up to a Black Panther selling Panther newspapers.*

ACTOR 1

Say, brother . . . let me have one of those papers, will ya?

How much? . . . A quarter? . . . Square business. . . . Here ya are . . .

Say, brother . . . you Panthers sell papers just like the Muslims . . . don't cha? You learned to do that from them? Nawh . . . ya didn't? . . . Then where did you learn it from?

Now, look, brother . . . I ain't tryin' to hassle you . . . I think that brothers should learn from brothers.

But I just heard that your boss, Eldridge Cleaver, say that the Muslims were counterrevolutionary . . . or somethin' like that . . . and I was wonderin' . . . if you patternin' your newspaper methods after the Muslims because you want them to become real revolutionaries like you . . .

(ACTOR 2 *comes up*)

ACTOR 2

(To Panther)

Say, man . . . I just read Cleaver's Manifesto . . . wow
. . . man. What do you think of that?

ACTOR 1

Of what?

ACTOR 2

Didn't you know? . . . Cleaver's callin' for a race war
between black people and whites.

ACTOR 1

Wow . . . man . . . we can get the shit on now.

ACTOR 2

Maybe you can, Home . . . but it seems to me that
Cleaver's doin' the writin' 'n talkin' . . . and my ass is
over here doin' the fightin' in this race war.

ACTOR 1

Hey, that's right . . . why he do that?

ACTOR 2

He did it to make a political threat against whites who
have Bobby Seale jammed up.

ACTOR 1

Bobby who?

ACTOR 2

Never mind, man . . . you outta it . . . but our ass gotta
do the fightin' . . . right, brother Panther?

ACTOR 1

That don't sound too cool to me. . . . I ain't even got a
rod, yet.

[142]

ACTOR 2

Well you better get one, Captain. Cause the word's about to be given.

ACTOR 1

Damn . . . hey, Panther . . . is the Muslims, SNCC, CORE, The NAACP, The Cultural Nationalists, The Urban League, The Preachers and the other Black people in this too?

ACTOR 2

War is war . . . brother.

ACTOR 1

Damn . . . why ya have to go an' call it now . . . I just about got mah short paid for . . . I was gonna cool it this summer . . . now I gotta take me out a loan to get me some guns. . . . Hey, man . . . give me another one of those papers. I gotta show this mess to mah ole lady.

etc., etc., etc. . . .

May, 1970

STREET SOUNDS

(Dialogues with Black Existence)

THE PEOPLE

PIGS
HARLEM POLITICIAN
DOPE SELLER
SOUL SISTER
BLACK REVOLUTIONARY ARTIST
BLACK DEE JAY
CORNER BROTHER
LOVER MAN
MAD DAWG
SEDUCED & ABANDONED
TRAFFIC MAN
ERRAND BOY
SCRAPBOOK KEEPER
NON-IDEOLOGICAL NIGGERS
THE BOWLER
WOMAN POET
THE THIEF
THE LIAR
WORKIN' MAN
FUN LOVIN'
THE REMEMBERER
THE QUITTER
THE LOVED ONE
THE DOUBTER
THE EXPLAINER
THE RECLUSE

THE GROOVER
WILD CHILE
BLACK CRITIC
THE RECONCILED
THE VIRGIN
THE LOSER
YOUNG WEST INDIAN REVOLUTIONARY POET
THE GENIUS
THE THEORIST
FRIED BRAINS
WAITING
THE RAPPER
BEWILDERED
HARLEM MOTHER

STREET SOUNDS *was first performed at La Mama Experimental Theater Club in New York City by La Mama's GPA Nucleus, Hugh Gittens, Director, in October 1970. Sets by Charles Terel; lighting by David Adams.*

The cast members and their roles are as follows:

PIGS	LAWRENCE SELLARS, JOHN O'SHAUNESSY
HARLEM POLITICIAN	NORMAN GIBBS
DOPE SELLER	GARRETTE MORRIS
SOUL SISTER	VICKIE THOMAS
BLACK REVOLUTIONARY ARTIST	ROBERT STOCKING
BLACK DEE JAY	RODNEY CLEGHORNE
CORNER BROTHER	GARRETTE MORRIS
LOVER MAN	GARRETTE MORRIS
MAD DAWG	RONALD BALLARD
SEDUCED & ABANDONED	NORMA DARDEN
TRAFFIC MAN	RONALD BALLARD
ERRAND BOY	JAY FLETCHER
SCRAPBOOK KEEPER	CHARLES PEGUES

NON-IDEOLOGICAL NIGGERS	ROBERT STOCKING,
	PATRICIA GAUL
THE BOWLER	REDVERA JEANMARIE
WOMAN POET	MARY ALICE
THE THIEF	JAY FLETCHER
THE LIAR	BRUCE LEVINE
WORKIN' MAN	GARRETTE MORRIS
FUN LOVIN'	BACI
THE REMEMBERER	ANTONY BASSAE
THE QUITTER	BARBARA MONTGOMERY
THE LOVED ONE	VICKIE THOMAS
THE DOUBTER	NORMAN GIBBS
THE EXPLAINER	REDVERA JEANMARIE
THE RECLUSE	NORMAN GIBBS
THE GROOVER	MARY ALICE
WILD CHILE	ALEXIS
BLACK CRITIC	LAWRENCE HOPPER
THE RECONCILED	MARY ALICE
THE VIRGIN	STEPHANIE FLAGG
THE LOSER	JAY FLETCHER
YOUNG WEST INDIAN	
REVOLUTIONARY POET	NORMAN GIBBS
THE GENIUS	RODNEY CLEGHORNE
THE THEORIST	ROBERT STOCKING
FRIED BRAINS	BACI
WAITING	BARBARA MONTGOMERY
THE RAPPER	LAWRENCE HOPPER
BEWILDERED	CHARLES PEGUES
HARLEM MOTHER	ROBERT STOCKING

PIG

Yeah . . . beat him . . . beat his ass . . . beat his ass,
I say . . . yeah . . . give it to him . . . crack his damn
ribs. Break the bastard's head! Use your club more . . .
yeah . . . like that . . . like that. Don't forget your hose
. . . yeah . . . that's right . . . Ooooooo Jesus! . .

the blood. Christ! . . . you're give'n that boy just what he deserves . . . the Black Panther . . . the black nigger . . . the Black protestor . . . the Black student . . . the Black bastard. . . . Makes me mad just to think about him callin' us a pig. . . . Yeah! . . . work him over, Murphy . . . punch him! . . . I don't care how he looks when he gets to court . . . say he got hit by a flyin' brick. . . . Beat his nigger ass good. . . . Good! . . . Oink oink oink oink oink oink oink oink . . .

HARLEM POLITICIAN

So I take a little graft . . . so what . . . my constituents know me. They know my record on Civil Rights. They know what I've done for them down through the years. . . . They know that I'm their man . . . a *race* man . . . and I can be counted upon when the goin' gets rough. That's why they return me to office one term after another. That's why I've got Harlem sewed up. And have had it in my pocket all these years . . . and will continue to keep it that way. They know to vote for me. And they do. Whatever happens they have me looking after their interests . . . they can bank on that . . . so that's why they vote me in . . . and maybe . . . maybe it'll do 'em some good.

DOPE SELLER

Sure I sell shit . . . pure junk with only a little talcum and other stuff in it to whoever wants to buy it. I can't see anything wrong with it . . . if that's what they want . . . I have it for them. So what if it's poison. So what if it destroys lives and turns the community into a spiritual ghost town. It's what they have to have . . . and I'm the dude who's got what they want. Yeah . . . anything for any kind of high. What can I get you? Huh? Huh? A nickel bag? Need a needle? What about a snort or two of some of this white ice that'll freeze your skull. . . . Sure I sell shit . . . every day of the week. I know what

everybody says . . . but if I didn't get their money somebody else would move in and take care of grand theft
business . . . and besides . . . I know I can do 'em some
good.

SOUL SISTER

Soul Sister . . . that's what they say I am. Their soul
sister. But I dunno . . . sometimes I feel so drug I don't
see how anybody can see any soul or anything else in
me. . . . In fact I just want them to keep their distance,
all of them, especially those jive-ass nigger men. Always
claimin' what I got . . . nigger men always sayin': "Yeah
. . . sister's got the best turd cutter in the world, Jim!"
. . . Yeah . . . always braggin' and puttin' it off on me
. . . like they did somethin' to make me have the super
booty they say I have . . . sheet . . . they ain't give it
to me . . . that's fo' real. Nigger men . . . even those
who say they Black . . . all they want to do is come in
you . . . yeah get their nuts off. Give me big bellies and
a lot of "It ain't mine," "I ain't got nothin' ta do wit' it."
Sheet . . . I got their soul sister for them. . . . They can
take it and do what they can with it. . . . Ha ha . . .
maybe it'll do 'em some good.

BLACK REVOLUTIONARY ARTIST

We have a country of the mind, my brothers. . . . We
have a country of the mind that is Black terrain. We pull
our ways up our intellect's insurmountable peaks . . .
we loaf in its gray depressions . . . we, ourselves, are
parched from the endless safaris across our brain's vast
expanse. We guerrillas of the psyche and spirit command
its ridges and gullies. We control the lines of communication. It is our country of the mind that we must take back
from Europe, my brothers. From the Euro-beast nations.
Our minds and spirits locked-up in their libraries, muse-
ums, schools and temples. We must wage revolution in
our spiritual/intellectual/cultural nation—which will lib-

erate our mind from the oppressor and cause our Black imagination self-determination to create the future. A revolution. A cosmic revolution that will liberate the highest potential of nationhood in the universe.

BLACK DEE JAY

Yeah . . . and this is your Jivin' Jones' hippy dippy SOUL hour . . . Yeah! . . . Jivin' Jones . . . the hip one! . . . Jivin' Jones . . . brought to you by the Primitive Products Co. . . . created by your friendly neighborhood Jew . . . Abe Goldblatt . . . Mr. Abe gives you a full line of Afro hair products . . . Afro Keep, Afro Cool, Afro Out and Afro Keen. For all you groovy, *together* Black folks. Swingin'. Yeah . . . the Jivin' Jones hip SOUL hour. Remember . . . Afro Primitive Products . . . 'cause Mr. Abe says "BLACK MEANS BUY!" . . . Hit it! The Jivin' Jones SOUL hour. Yeah! Niggers got more records than books . . . yeah, dance your lives away . . . yeah . . . Jivin' Jones will tell you, listen Black people . . . while you jive your lives away.

CORNER BROTHER

Hey, whiteboy! . . . give me ah quarter so I can get downtown, huh? Ya got ah quarter, man? You don't . . . ah man . . . don't come with dat shit! . . . I know you got ah quarter so I can get downtown, man . . . you workin' . . . ain't cha? All you whities got a hame . . . or a hustle . . . or some way to get some dough. Huh? . . . How you sound, man? How you sound? What makes you think I'm gonna buy some wine? What makes you think dat? Ah, man . . . you think dat, huh? Ahhh . . . man . . . it ain't none of yo business. You white sonna bitch! Just give me a quarter before I bust you in you fukkin' white mouf, mathafukker! . . . Just give it up! . . . you jive-ass gray chump . . . give it up, punk! . . . Give it all here . . . 'n shut yo pale mathafukkin' no quarter givin' ass!

I love you, baby. You know that, don't you? Don't you
know that, baby? Huh, baby? Sure you do. You know
I love you, baby. Yeah . . . can't help myself when it
comes down on me. Yeah. When I see you . . . see you,
mamma . . . fine little mamma . . . I just wants to hold
you in my arms and kiss your beautiful black face.
Oeeewww . . . baby. I sure dig that sexy natural. Let
me smell ya . . . Ummmm . . . mamma. Too tough. Oh
yes, indeed. Yeah . . . I love you, baby. Come on . . .
come on . . . yeah. Lil mamma . . . come on. You really
the one fo' me. The one and only, baby. First time I laid
eyes on you I said to myself that you was the one fo' me.
Yeah . . . baby. Yeah . . . baby . . . Uhmmm . . .

That's bullshit! BULLSHIT! . . . Don't try an' put that
off on me, man. I ain't gonna carry that. What the fuck
you mean? Don't be sayin' that shit! I ain't gonna go for
it. Nawh. That's bullshit, man. You didn't hear me say
that. Nawh. Nawh, ya didn't! Didn't nothin' like that come
out of my mouf. I ain't no fool, man. You can't run that
jive on me. I just ain't gonna deal with it, that's all. When
did you hear me say that? You sure are somethin', man.
I wouldn't think that of you. And you better not think it
of me. This just ain't gonna work . . . ya hear? Me always bein' made out to be the bad guy. I ain't gonna
stand for it. Don't be talkin' that shit. Just knock off the
bullshit!

You think I'm crazy, don't ya? . . . Don't ya? . . . Well
I may be . . . and I may be not. . . . Hee ha ha . . .
got cha fooled, ain't I? Just 'cause you see me blowin' this
tin police whistle and swingin' this fake head-whuppin'
stick and directin' traffic with my play badge on, wearin'

my dirty sneakers and greasy officer's cap . . . don't make
me out to be crazy . . . understand? . . . I'm just takin'
care of . . . uhmmm . . . that's why I'm blowin' this
whistle in the middle of the street fo'. And tellin' this
here traffic where to go. It's my job. Mine! Well, nobody
had to give it to me . . . but somebody did. Long time
ago. And I'm the only one who knows who that was. So
if you'll excuse me . . . I'll get back to work. The traffic's
backin' up on the uptown side of the street. Now looka
here . . . I know what you thinkin' an' all . . . an' it's
confused thinkin'. I'm a professional man . . . just doin'
my job. Don't be thinkin' I'm crazy. Crazy folks is locked
up where they should be. They ain't out here doin' ser-
vices to mankind. You can understand that, can't you?
. . . Good. Now I got to get back to work . . . fo' my
boss calls me up.

SEDUCED & ABANDONED

But why? . . . Why? . . . I love you. . . . But why you
do this to me? Why? Why? . . . Do I deserve this? Is
this right? I ain't much to look at. We both always knew
that. I know I'm awkward and clumsy . . . but you said
you loved me. I'm black with a flat, wide nose and big
lips. You said you admired me because of my mind . . .
ha ha . . . You married me because of my ability to
understand you, you said. I didn't want a child. I only
wanted to be with you and for us to go on together. Oh,
baby . . . oh, baby . . . please please please . . . don't
do this to me . . . Oh, baby . . . please. I'm not just
askin' for me . . . My ego ain't that much, honey, really.
Remember . . . I've even worked since we been together
so that you could keep doin' the things you need to do.
So I'm not just askin' for me. . . . Not really for me,
honey. It's for you . . . for you yourself. How can you
be the man you always said you wanted to be if you do
this . . . if you abandon me and our baby . . . oh, baby

[151]

. . . I love you so much and you're doin' this to us . . . I can't think anymore . . . it's too much for me. . . . But I want to ask you . . . Why? . . . Why? I know that we'll make it . . . our baby and me . . . but makin' it ain't where it's at, baby. That's one of your sayin's. Remember how well you've taught me? Makin' it ain't where it's at . . . it's bein' who you are and what you are . . . a man . . . or tryin' to be. Remember? Oh, man, I don't like to cry . . . don't make me . . . don't make me, baby. Why? Why . . . you make me want to die at such an early age, man.

ERRAND BOY

Hey, man . . . How ya doin'? Ain't seen you in a long, long time, man. Where you been? . . . Lots of places, huh? . . . I thought you were dead, man. Ain't seen you in so long. You been in the service, huh? And in jail. . . . Well, I figured that. . . . And you been livin' other places. Yeah. I figured. . . . But you lookin' good, man. Put on so much weight. . . . But it looks good on ya, ya understand? . . . Hey, ya want me to go to the store for you or somethin'? Yeah . . . I'm doin' okay. Makin' it, ya know. Most of the guys that we usta swing with are gone, man. In jail, on wine or scag . . . or in their graves . . . Things have changed a lot, man. Can't even recognize the old corner. The Heat Wave's gone. So is the Cotton Bowl. . . . All the places where we usta swing, man. The whole neighborhood's torn up. . . . Can't even make a livin' round here, man . . . but we never could, right? . . . Say, can I go to the store for you? . . . Nawh, man . . . I don't see him no more . . . Ha ha . . . remember when you two cats usta fight all the time? You never did beat him . . . did you? But you and him sure had some boss fights. . . . When I run into some of the old studs sometimes . . . sometimes when we have a bottle we talk about you and him and the other guys and wonder whatever happened to them. You don't look like you doin' so

[152]

bad . . . but most of the rest of us . . . wow . . . a
wipe out, brother. . . . Hey, man, can I get anything
at the store fo' you?

This is the scrapbook of my accomplishments. Yes, it's
true, brothers, that I am a young Black man but I know
that I'll be an important Black man. . . . I have a destiny to fulfill . . . a fate too that is determined by the
Black Gods . . . so I wish to chronicle my every effort.
. . . The Black man needs heroes, brothers . . . and I,
of course, shall be one of the greater Black heroes, so the
Black World needs me. We must document our past,
brothers, and examine our present. . . . You can quote
me on that. . . . Yes, brothers. My scrapbook will not
only contain my ideas, memories, opinions . . . but my
likeness, my history, my presence . . . but, too, it will
be an historical record of my impact upon Black people's
history, and the world's thinking. Negroes got more records than books . . . yawhl . . . but our books are rele-
vant . . . when they are about something important . . .
like me. Yes, brothers. A scrapbook of me. Your leader.
Your spokesman. Your enlightened teacher. All Praises
Due the Black man, brothers . . . and certainly, All
Praises Due Me.

Why, certainly . . . I am Black and non-ideological. You
mean to say that my skin denotes an inherent political,
economic and national philosophy? I must say . . . I
cannot go along with that. Indeed, I am uncommitted
to any system of ideas—completely—as well as being a
member of the colored peoples one hundred percent, of
course. It's simple, you see. My non-alignment with reality
is quite evident and explainable . . . my being Black and
non-committed to any political truths . . . well, it's not
as unrealistic as it may appear, you see, old chap.

Black is more to me than a political/cultural/sociological/ psychological/existential matrix, my brother . . . its spiritual essence transcends the mere limitations of the definable. . . . To me, to be without an entrapping set of dogmas is freedom of the highest order. It is the single life style which expresses the true and natural state of non-involved man . . . non-encumbered human. As a black man it is the only viewpoint I can take . . . no, not that of a vegetable . . . but as a free-floating individual cognizant of the dynamics of free choice, free will and free pussy . . . being that my wife is white.

BLACK WRITER

You see, man . . . I got this dream, man. You know I've had it for a long time, man. Yeah . . . that's to be a writer . . . yeah, a writer, man. And I've lived this dream, man . . . lived it for the past couple years. As soon as I got out of the service and got home I started in writing this novel. I didn't know what a job it would be at first, but I got hung up in it, you see. At first I would just write so much . . . and then show it to my girl, or my mother and dad. And then I found myself working more and more on it. Man, I didn't even see my friends much, cause I was workin' on this novel. I still got some checks from the service and I took a few night courses in English and writing so that they would send me more checks, so I didn't have to work right away. And my girl thought I was crazy. Yeah, she did. "Why you wastin' your time doin' that for?" she would say. And I'd tell her about my dream. Tell her all about it. Tell her how I was gonna finish my novel. Then begin another I had in my head. And get them published in hardback and be a real author. And show everybody. Show my family who was thinkin' I was crazy like my girl thought I was. Show all my old partners who had put me down for bein' strange. I'd show them. But, man, the more I wrote . . . the more I had to write . . . and the more I did write.

I wrote and wrote . . . then my girl didn't call anymore
. . . and when I had time to call her she didn't answer
her phone. And my mother stopped speaking to me. And
my ole man just turned his back on me when I walked
through the room. . . . So I went out and got a job at
the post office. . . . I drive a Mustang now . . . with
only thirty more payments on it to go. And I locked up
the room where I used to write. Didn't touch anything
in there. Just locked it up with all my notes, papers and
books in it. . . . Maybe it'll become the nursery . . .
now that I'm married to my girl; and my mother is smiling . . . but I drink myself into a stupor each night with
my dad as we sit in front of the TV . . . I guess I'm
happy, man . . . cause I don't dream at all . . . no
more.

THE BOWLER

We met in the bowlin' alley. I go Tuesdays, Wednesdays
and Thursdays . . . at night. Our club's in the league.
"The Vampers" . . . you've probably heard of us . . .
hee ha ha . . . yeah . . . we down there all the time.
Don't play for no high stakes. Just for relaxation, rec-
reation and sociability . . . ha ha . . . you understand?
I'm sorta like the captain of the team . . . when the real
captain ain't around . . . ha ha . . . so I kinda take
charge of things. Well, I met this woman. I call her a
woman cause she's a little older than me . . . but lookin'
good. I meet a lot of them down at the alley. They come
around to have some fun. And most of them can't bowl
so good, so I help them out . . . you know what I mean?
Well, we hit it off from the start. And she meets me every
Tuesday, Wednesday and Thursday night after that. And
I keep showin' her how to play the game. And I don't
mind none, you understand? She's lookin' good, no jive.
It went on for a month. Then we met when we wasn't
playin'. On Mondays, Fridays, Saturdays . . . and even
Sundays. And one thing led to another. You know what

I mean, don't cha? She was divorced. Was a nurse. Drove a lil' "T" Bird and was buyin' a house in the negro suburbs where her son and she lived. We really hit it off. Got married almost two months to the day of when we first met. That sure was somethin' . . . hee ha ha . . . you remember the wedding, right? Really jive. And I moved in with her. That was three months ago. So now, man, I'd like you as a buddy to come down to court and testify in my behalf as to my character . . . hee ha ha. . . . Yeah . . . she wants an annulment. . . . Yeah, man, I'm serious! . . . ha ha . . . What? Nawh, brother, I don't bowl no more.

WOMAN POET

Honey . . . women poets are different from men poets. Yes, I know that! But you know that's not what I mean. What I mean is that men have . . . well they have something that women don't have. No! I don't mean that. Please. Be serious with me about this. Now, no foolin' now. You as a man know . . . please please . . . don't interrupt! You as a man know as I know as a woman that men have bigger egos than women. Wait, I'm not insulting you. I'm just stating a fact. Yes, a fact! Men do things like write and play music and do art on a totally different basis than women. Maybe it's not all ego. . . . What? . . . You're not going to use that argument, are you? Of course there is such a thing as an ego. . . . Ohhh . . . let's forget that. Maybe it's only male ambition . . . or something. It's not just because women have babies and all that stuff . . . and because of the social climate that makes females create less observable art than men. . . . Ohhh . . . you're acting just like a man . . . a Black one at that! It's just that women are different, baby. I know you know that we're different. I'm not talking about that; you know that! It's just that women, it doesn't seem, are interested in turning out one piece of art after another, one poem after another . . . and forever beating their

chests or breasts about it and living off the reputations
that art makes for them. We women artists are different
that's all . . . no, I don't know exactly how or why. But
we're different. And should be accepted for our unique-
ness. . . . What did you say? . . . No, I'm sorry, dear,
I'm still not ready to have children yet.

THE THIEF

I'm gonna rip that mathafukker's typewriter off. That's
what I'm gonna do. I can hear him typin' every night and
morning. He must go out in the afternoons . . . cause
I don't hear him none. Maybe he's sleepin'. But does he
sleep in the afternoon as well as at night after he finishes
typing? Nawh . . . he can't be sleepin' all that much. It
seems as if I've heard his footsteps go down the stairs
in the afternoon. But I can't always be certain. This scag
they been sellin' me lately makes me hear funny. But I can
hear him typin' now. Wonder what he's doin'? Never
could figure out how anybody could just sit down all day
and do nothin' 'cept pick at a typewriter. Sure wish I
had me a typewriter . . . I'd sell it and get me somethin'
to get high on. That's what I'd do. Just you wait. As soon
as he goes out I'm gonna climb out this window, crawl
along the window ledge to his window, get into his place
. . . and cop his typewriter. He won't even know who
did it. He don't even know me. I'll let myself out by his
door and then kick it in so he'll think I came in that way.
Yeah, that's what I'll do. That nigger don't need a typewriter anyway. Who he think he is anyway? Black people
are natural . . the they don't need machines and stuff like
dat to do what they got to do. Wait . . . I hear his door
opening. He's going down the stairs. Well . . . I better
get to work. . . . Damn . . . I'm gonna get me enough
shit to hold me for a day or two.

THE LIAR

I always get in trouble tellin' the truth. Yes, the truth, of all things. Surprised? You should be. Now listen. No matter how I attempt to use my mouth it falls open and out comes, you know what I am going to say already, the truth. No lie. Even when I lie, I lie truthfully. Truth is a great handicap, you know. No lie. A great great handicap. Here I am. In the prime of life I face the world. I'm no stranger to experience. No passing acquaintance to reality. I can say with my usual candid self that I always say what I always say. And that's usually wrong, of course. People don't like to hear what they don't like to hear. Upsets them. Causes bad vibrations. They get into a thing with you. No lie. Like, "Mind your business!" Or, "Shut up!" And, "You're a big mouth!" Shucks . . . I'm only being me. You know what? From now on I'm not going to tell the truth at all. I've decided that this is the best course for all concerned. I find the world isn't ready for the truth yet. So I'm going to change my tactics completely. From now on I'm going to be known as the biggest liar around. That's right, a really thorough and complete liar. Only thing though . . . and nobody will know it but me . . . I am going to think the truth whatever happens.

NEW NEGRO PUBLISHER

You see . . . the way that I see it is if we print a half a million copies . . . our return will be over a million. Yessirreee . . . a million stone-cold dollars. We got everything going for us. The material, the artwork inside, which is unbelievable in itself. The writing is an inspiration! I wouldn't doubt that after the art alone is seen that the President himself . . . yes, the President of the United States . . . will be calling up for his orders for himself and his friends. It's a class negro publication, you understand? We got our product on the best lists. The President's, the F.B.I., the U.S.I.A., the Voice of America, the C.I.A., the U.S. Government Library Service and all the colleges and universities . . . throughout the world!

That's amazing, ain't it? We got an advance order of three hundred thousand. Before the book's even seen. I've left no stone unturned. This isn't a jive outfit. That's why I'm affiliated with all the major negro business organizations across the country. The banks and government know you're takin' care of business when you are hooked up in a real business sense. You dig? So now all I need now is to get the books printed. That's all . . . and I'll have the money any day now for that. It's all a matter of time. Just wait . . . you'll see. Any day now I'll find it feasible to produce those half million copies . . . and I'll expedite all the orders. I got fourteen girls standing by this very moment ready to lick the stamps and fold flaps. I got a staff of forty that will move on a moment's notice. It won't be long now. Any day now . . . say, brother, would you like to take out an advance subscription for only twelve bucks?

WORKIN' MAN

Yeah . . . I've been workin' on this job for years. My whole family does, almost, at least my mother and sisters with me. I'm a foreman now. Make pretty good bread. . . . Since we got a union now . . . tryin' to buy me a house . . . if my F.H.A. loan ever comes through. If you had'a seen me fifteen years ago you wouldn't never have thought you'd be talkin' to me now. Man . . . I was a bad nigger. Yeah. I was bad. And everybody knew it. I was always in trouble. In jail for fightin' and cuttin' niggers, in reform school for robbin' and stealin'—from white men, brother—I knew what Black Power was before some college kids began gettin' diarrhea of the lip. I was out of work, bummin' around, no prospects. I was even so bad in school that I didn't learn much. Hardly how to read and write. It was somethin' else, man. Got so bad that the Army wouldn't even take me. I couldn't even join, man. I was at a pretty low ebb. Couldn't steal much, nobody wanted me around. My crime partner, Tootsie,

and me were trapped . . . trapped inside of ourselves,
inside our surroundings, inside our experience. Yeah,
those sound like some good words, you understand? I can
rap them some . . . although I can't write them so good.
But I wanted to give you an idea of how bad things were
for me. I had just about had it. My sisters were down on
me, my brother went to the Army for life, but Mom got
me a job where she worked. And that's where I've been
since. Didn't know I could or would work that hard and
steady. I still drank and ran around and did other things
but I worked. Tootsie didn't work steady but we still ran
together. Even pulled an occasional job. And I took some
night courses . . . to help me out. And I became foreman after a while. And I grew fat. Tootsie got hisself
killed last year by some broad's husband . . . and now
I'm scared to stay out late at night because my ole lady's
threatened to lock me out and not let me in . . . Damn
. . . I wonder what the next twenty years is going to
be like.

FUN LOVIN'

Hey, baby . . . why don't you go with me? . . . You
ain't got nothin' to do right now . . . and I haven't
nothin' to do that I can't do it with you. My ole man's
out chasin' a quarter . . . and I saw your ole lady goin'
to the hairdresser. I told her to wait for me there until
I came back. Is that okay, huh? I dig the way you walk,
man. If I was a right-actin' sister I wouldn't go into this,
you understand . . . but you know I ain't right-actin'.
Never been. That's what you like about me. C'mon . . .
it's going to be a nice afternoon. We always have a good
time, don't we? No strings. Clean. It's been that way for
the past year and a half . . . hasn't it? I dig the way
you talk, baby. And how you feel in bed beside me. You
know how to love me like a woman should be loved. And
you know just what to say, honey. I got some good grass
. . . ummm . . . whew! . . . Santa Fe Green. So let's

stop and get some grapes . . . how bout port? . . . Oh, that's right, you do like that old dry stuff. . . . But I dig drinkin' with you, my man. . . . In fact I like lots of things about you. . . . Oh, good, you're smilin'.

THE REMEMBERER

Yes. I knew her. I knew all the great ones. But she was the greatest. Yes. I knew Josephine. And my my . . . wasn't she just terrific? So glamorous . . . so gorgeous. I can see her now sweeping down the aisle in one of her special outfits. It was marvelous to behold . . . I can tell you that. Everything she did was queenlike. Josephine was a star among stars. A near goddess. I used to work for her. Yes, I did. When she used to come to town and play at the Earl I usta be her maid. That's right. She'd call me up. (I'd be working down in South Philly doin' maid work at the wop whorehouse.) "Gertrude," that's what she'd call me. None of that "Gertie" stuff. "Gertrude," she'd say. "Come help me out, won't you, dear?" And I'd work for her as long as she was in town. And I even came to the Big Apple with her several times. Never did stay with her too much though . . . she moved too fast and far for me. And I made most of my money takin' care of the wop's place. But I was always ready to help out Josie. She was a dear. The times we had together . . . uummmm uummmm . . . I could really tell you some stories. I could write a book, you know. Yes, I could really tell some things if I opened up and let fly. But she's still alive. Yes, alive and well and struggling to stay alive in Europe . . . ha ha . . . Never can tell what harm my memories could cause her. Hell, I'd cut off my breasts before I'd hurt Josie. So I just keep what I know to myself; I tell my grandchildren stories, sometimes. And my little friends like you. And late at night when no one's around . . . sometimes I take out old pictures and show programs and spread my memories out on the bed.

School's okay. It has its advantages. Can't complain about it, really. I get loans to go and grants and other things. Work in the Black Students' Union; started it and run it, really. That's right, I'm a pretty together sister. But the students aren't too together, not yet. They're getting better now, but they have a long way to go. I got most of the brothers and sisters on our campus out of those fraternities and sororities. That was a big accomplishment. Started a Black Community Involvement program. Even had some on-going programs in the ghetto, completely staffed by B.S.U. members. Then we began to take over student government. Started running for office, voting in blacks and getting some of the student government money for our use. It was pretty together . . . some of the things we did. We started takin' care of business. Not many of us smoked as much pot as before. And L.S.D. almost disappeared from our circle. Most of the brothers and sisters really began takin' care of business except those few left in the frats. . . . Then Black Power came on campus . . . that was a fight . . . then Black Studies . . . it's a long story . . . and it's been a hard fight. We lost some brothers and sisters. Yes, they went back into the frats. Six sisters began fryin' their heads again. A few got shot by National Guardsmen and State Troopers . . . sixty are in jail . . . and one of our main revolutionary brothers blew his thumbnail off tryin' to activate a bomb in the women's gym. And school will be delayed in initiating a new semester . . . the administration building was burned down . . . with four classroom buildings. It's good to be a Black Student these days . . . never dull for a second . . . and it has so many advantages. Makes a leader out of you. . . . Currently, I'm pregnant. But next semester is another semester. Right on, brotherman! Just tryin' to be Black, yawhl . . . that's all.

THE QUITTER

Don't try talking me out of it again. It's off! . . . Through!
There's no turning back now. Whatever you say will fall
on deaf ears. I've had all that a human body can take
. . . and more. I'm through! This is the end . . . I am
leaving. You're bad. Your evil ways are more than I can
stand. I've taken too much of your crap! . . . Yes, I said
it. Shit! You're not a fit human being to live with. That's
right, not fit! Your own mother couldn't live in the same
house with you. God! . . . I've tried to live with this
goddamn man. Lord knows I've tried to make it. I'm
only a weak little old pore/ass black woman. It would
take Hannibal . . . his momma . . . and his momma's
elephants to make it with you, honey. . . . So, 'bye. . . .
What? Don't slam the door as I go out? . . . Now listen
here, man. Don't you be orderin' me around. What? . . .
You want me to tone down my voice? YOU WANT ME
TO TONE DOWN MY VOICE? . . . I ain't your woman
. . . no more. You got no right to be givin' me orders.
Don't be tellin' me what to do, man. I ain't going anywhere. Do you hear? Nowhere! You don't be tellin' me
when I come or when I go. . . . Wha? . . . Don't you
say that! . . . You just keep quiet . . . or I'm leaving.

THE LOVED ONE

Darling, I've got something to tell you. Now I want you
to listen, you hear? It won't take long. Just give me a
minute to compose myself. What I have to say isn't exactly easy. Not at all it isn't. So I want you to listen to
me, and give me a chance. Wait. Just wait. In a minute
it'll all be over, darling. Then we can do what we have
to do. It'll be out and said . . . and that'll be that. You
see what I have to say will hurt me as much or more than
it will hurt you. But it has to be said. It has to get out.
It's pushing against my insides, pressing and coming up
like vomit and my throat cannot hold the filth any longer.

. . . Dear? . . . What are you laughing at? . . . Nothing, you say? Now you're not going to start that stuff about me being romantic, are you? . . . Well, I should think not. . . . Please be serious for once. . . . Just let me tell you. . . . Darling, I am going to have an abortion. . . . Yes, I'm getting an abortion. . . . Did you hear me? . . . I said did you hear me? . . . I said did you hear me? . . . You did? . . . Well? . . . Well? . . . I assume that you have nothing to say. You have? You have something to say. . . . Oh? . . . I see. You think it's a good idea. . . . I see. . . . Yes, darling, I see . . . What? . . . What am I crying for? . . . Me crying? . . . Ha ha . . . how funny. . . . But, yes, I guess these are tears rolling from my eyes. It's funny, that's all. Just strange. . . . What? . . . Oh, I once thought that you loved me.

THE DOUBTER

Those phonies. . . . Look at them. With their Afros and dashikis and tikis. They *have* to be the blackest things in town . . . if you look at them. That's right, the blackest things in town now but everybody knows that they had white wives. Not that that's the worst thing in the world. But look at them today and there's not a hint of their past. The past is as dead to them as the buffalo on the nickel. That's right. It's hard to say . . . but it has to be said. It's hard to listen to . . . but listen we must. But we cannot be carried away by prejudice. Not Black being prejudiced against other Blacks. A man's past is his past. What one does in the ignorance of youth cannot be held against him when he matures, and sincerely attempts to change his ways. But those hypocrites always harping on their high standards of morals. Their forever pronouncing superior values and their stances of uprightness. . . . At least I never hid my white bitches . . . that's when I was into that, ya know . . . and I ain't never married one. But I say again, don't hold a man's past against him.

Especially if he's changed direction for the better, for Blackness, for instance. But remember what I say . . . all my wives have been Black . . . that's a fact. So when you look for Black people look for tried-and-true Black people . . . and not phonies that have white pasts.

THE EXPLAINER

What can I do, man? She's white . . . I know that. I know that she's white. But she's my ole lady. . . . Can you get to that? . . . You can? Good . . . but you can't see how I can be with her. Yeah, I know how you feel, man, but there's things you don't see. What? What are they? Well now looka here, man. What can I do? I don't care if her daddy's oppressing me. Damn . . . he's doing that to everybody, ain't he? And I don't care what you say about her sapping my will to fight. . . . Man . . . you don't know the fighting I had to do to get her. . . . And you sure don't know the troubles I've seen to keep her. . . . And I don't care about the political, economic and social situation . . . neither about the international one. She's my woman. . . . That's all there is to that. My woman. And I ain't allowin' no two-cent no-count nigger to talk me out of her.

THE RECLUSE

. . . to be left alone. That's right. All I want is to be left alone. That's all . . . to be left alone . . . yeah, if I could only get that. If I could only get it. . . . That's all I want is just to be left alone. Really. Anything that anybody wants to do is groovy with me. It's cool, man. . . . Really. Go ahead and do your thing, champ. Those are my mottos, brother. I'll make 'em slogans any day. Right? Cause all I want is to be left alone. . . . I ain't complainin', none at all, for whatever somebody done in the past. The past is the past. . . . It's as dark as I am. . . . Everything's everything. It's okay, chief. . . . Nothin' to worry about. It's cool. It's all right. . . . No bother at all. Don't lose your cool, prez. Get yourself together . . . if that's what you want, bossman. . . . Yessir . . . it's all right with me. Boss, hoss. Anything you say. Let us let bygones be bygones . . . right? . . . Cause all I want is to be left alone.

THE GROOVER

Ohhh . . . feel so good. Feel so good. . . . Ummm . . . feel for real about my soul thing . . . yeah . . . yeah . . . Oh, yeah . . . uummmm . . . sho is good, ya know. So good . . . ummmm . . . Oh, daddy, sock it to me. . . . Oh, yes, oh, yes . . . one more time . . . just one more time. Oh, yes, just one. . . . Daddy . . . ohhh . . . do it. Yes. Don't stop. Don't stop. It's so good . . . so good. Oh, honey . . . I just love the way you make me feel.

SLIGHTLY CONFUSED NEGRO

Yeah, my man, I make it with her even though I'm supposed to be her ole man's friend. Nawh, it doesn't bother my conscience none. Nawh, not at all. Well, look at it from my point of view: Now, I'm Black, ain't I? Why you takin' so long in answerin'? Good. That's obvious, sure. And her ole man's white, right? Yeah. White. Dig it. A white cat married to a black broad. And so I'm fuckin' her. Okay. What you want me to do? So I'm supposed to be his friend. And when his ole lady's horny we make it. Simple as that. You know no white cat can really be your friend, right? So what's wrong if I take off his black stuff when he's downtown? The bitch digs me more than she could ever dig that gray-assed sucker. Of course he's my friend. But you know, there are friends and there are friends. Why don't I take his woman for keeps? That's a good question, friend, but a stupid one. Man, I've got an ole lady already. Yeah, she's white. So what? And what do I think she's doin' right now? She's at home waiting for me, that's what. Why'd you ask, man? You

think you wise or somethin'? I don't see nothin' wrong
with screwin' that black bitch. She ain't even as Black
as she wants Black people to think she is. Rappin' Black
but sleepin' white. The bitch! At least everybody knows
I'm liberal. No, fool, not a Liberal . . . just liberal. Yeah,
I'm a liberal Black man. Not only in politics, you understand, but socially, culturally and sexually. Is there such
a thing? Certainly you see me standing here, don't you?
I have white friends and everything. I'm too mature and
sophisticated to get sucked in by racist arguments. I
made my choice, man. So what if I do fuck the bitch even
though she should be my ole lady. Shit. I never could get
along with a black bitch. My white old lady makes me
feel good. And screwin' my best white friend's black wife
makes me feel even better. Makes me get my nuts off.
. . . Everybody in our integrated circle of mod people
is with it, man. We're the Now Crowd.

WILD CHILE

Hi! . . . you know me, don't you? Well . . . it doesn't
matter . . . ha ha . . . you'll know me well . . . soon
enough. I'm crazy, you see. Crazy, or so they say. They?
. . . My friends, naturally . . . who else? A dizzy, crazy
chick . . . ha ha . . . That's what people say about me.
Even my friends. And I have some interesting friends.
Some of my friends are just around me to see what I do
next. . . . ha ha . . . it's a scream. Mostly I do it to my
husband. . . . No, do crazy things, that is. Not the other
thing; that I do too, call it doin' it. Though don't like to
do that too much . . . at least not with him, my husband.
But I scream some . . . and become hysterical, or act the
part . . . and cry . . . yes, like I'm doing now but more
so . . . oh oh oh . . . I cry a lot, sometimes. About
what? . . . oh oh oh . . . about everything and nothing.
Just everything! My not being a white lady, for one. My
not being rich and able to go to Capri whenever my
whims win me over. My not wanting to do it but having

inner compulsions to screw my girlfriends men . . .
ha ha . . . cause it's good, that's why . . . ha ha . . .
and I like to fuck . . . ha ha . . . Oeee . . . I said it
finally. You see, being that I am mad I can cuss out-
rageously . . . when I want to or desire attention or am
horny or feelin' funky or bein' nitty-gritty or just am
my negress baddest . . . yes, indeed, doo wop ah-dop
. . . oh oh oh . . . go slow, partner . . . I'm built close
and my skin is light and changes after a hard night of
Black men screwin' . . . cause my husband's white. . . .
Sho I'm sho . . . and life could be better for this little
Black girl, mister . . . you got a dime? And the time to
be with me, pleez? So I can sing or dance or entertain
you until I get tired of you, good night, sweet Jesus!

BLACK CRITIC

This type of expression just has got to stop! What you
do is not art, is not playwrighting or theater or anything
worthwhile. What do you think you're doing? Is something wrong with your mind? You're irresponsible! You're
not fulfilling any of the needs of the people that I can see.
Look at what you are doing to yourself and the negative
image of the race you create. We've had it hard enough.
We don't need to be showing *them* that side of us. It's
a disgrace, that's what it is. I wasn't raised that way.
Nobody I knew was. We were refined, man. And here
you are, at this late date, creating profanity, filth and
obscenity and displaying it to the masses, the Black people you so hypocritically harp about forever into the
future, as art and culture. You should be ashamed of
yourself, you cynical pimp! You hustler, you. You nigger
con man. The idea, those awful despairing figures you
deal with are grotesque and totally uncalled for and unrealistic. The work lacks range and its author fails to
demonstrate a measurable degree of responsibility to the
depiction of the unlettered masses. The very rudiments
of the fine art of dramaturgy are not adhered to. It's a

disgrace! Why should he be allowed to continue doing this filth and denigrating the people? Can we allow this not-so-disguised pornography to continue to infect the community? The people should not stand for it! They should take action and declaim this foul exploiter of the Black people, this bourgeois lackey of the establishment. This bandit of the masses' soul, this crusher of the people's spirit and diluter of their essence. As a theater craftsman it's as if he never heard of the word craft, not to mention art, as I've said previously, above. This so-called artist cannot continue doing just as he pleases with our Black Art. He's immoral. He takes all and gives nothing. Those dirty things he docs and says up on stage can't even be mentioned by responsible Black people and critics, like me. Black people, we are the ones to lose in this situation. Sure is a heavy game. I wanna thank you. Just doin' mah thang. Salaam, ahki. Kill the night blackness and groove.

THE RECONCILED

Where did I go when I left? Why do you ask? Best proof, I wasn't hanging around you waiting for you to treat me like your little dog. You were certainly happy when I left, weren't you? Or acted like it. Not happy? Only relieved that our constant fighting seemed over. Why do you say "seem"? It's over, isn't it? Oh, I shouldn't answer a question with another question. Can't you forget that corny sophomoric style for a minute? I did what I did and you have given sanction to my actions by your demonstrated disinterest. Yes, of course, you were disinterested. More than that. In fact, you even suggested that I leave. Yes, you did! Don't lie. I remember vividly your hurting me by your attitude and remarks. Yes, attitude and remarks. If it were only your attitude then you could be excused as being yourself, for you are generally a very mean-spirited individual. But the things that you said. Huh? . . . YES, I STAYED WITH A MAN! So what! Whatta you want to make of it? Yes, I did it and I'm glad. What, you thought that I couldn't get another man, right? You do think so little of me, don't you? I should have never come back to you. I should have stayed where I was. At least he appreciated me. And you don't, and you treat me just horrible. Yes, horrible. I'm glad I left. You don't deserve me! I'll never forgive you for that little tramp you were with. . . . Of course I love you. Why do you think I'm crying? Oh, man, all I want is you and to be yours. You make me go through some fantastic changes. But I guess I can't do without it, cause I'm back again.

THE OLDTIMER

Hey, how ya doin'? You lookin' good, sport. Can't say that life's disagreein' with you. Oh, I'm makin' it. Can't complain. Wouldn't do any good if I did, now would it, home boy? I just lay here . . . and check the world out. It's goin' by, ya know. Even though it don't look like it. Nawh, nawh, I ain't goin' nowhere. I'm here to stay. As long as the place stays. But they changin' things, you know? Freeways comin' through tearin' up the old neighborhood. Buildings goin' down, and not bein' put up again. Abandoned houses that are boarded up, the homes of winos, junkies and rats, catchin' fire and never bein' fixed up. The place is going down but I'm still hangin' in. This is my home, right? I grew up here. Grew up here just like you. But you only come back to visit. Not like me who is here to stay. I've seen people come and go. I've seen people born, die and live here year in and year out. The place ain't as nice as it was when we were kids growin' up around here. Most of the guys are gone— moved away like you, in the service, jail or dead. I don't know what happened to a lot of the gang. The girls all got knocked-up and set up homes, got married, went on the block or on welfare or turned into booze hounds. Yeah, I've seen it all happen. Man, I could write a book. Really could, you know. But that ain't my style, buddy-buddy. I just look and watch and stand. I wait for things to change. For the better? Well, it hasn't yet. But who knows. At least you know as it falls apart where you're at. And will be if there's anyplace left after a while. Well, it was good seein' you, old sport. Come on down again, anytime. I'll be here. Ya lookin' good. Where did you say you were livin' now? Oh. Well, that's nice. I always wanted to visit there. Wouldn't want to live there though for shit but always wanted to visit there. I'll give your best to everybody who's left. So long, brother.

THE VIRGIN

Ummm ummm . . . I ain't gonna give you none. No Ahuhn . . . No, not today. Or any day, for that matter. You don't even like me. You just want to get what you can from me. No you don't, you don't like me none. You always with my girlfriend, Buttercup. Yes, you are. Don't lie. I see you with her all the time and Buttercup tells me all about you. Did she tell me how good you make her feel? Get off me, boy! You too fresh. I want you to get off top of me. Get off me cause I ain't gonna give you any. And stop kissin' me on my neck . . . ha ha . . . it tickles. And it ain't gonna do you no good. Get off me! Don't you feel silly layin' on top of me on this couch? What if my mother or brother comes in? You supposed to be my play brother and you doin' this to me. You ain't gonna do nothin'. Stop! Keep your hands to yourself. You should be botherin' Buttercup, not me. She's gone away for the summer? Don't you do that! Don't you lift up my dress, man. Stop! You think you so funny, don't you? What's that hard thing? Oh! . . . I better not get pregnant, you know that, don't ya? And I better not catch you even lookin' at that old Buttercup again.

THE LOSER

Yeah . . . I went to jail for that cat. I wasn't mad at anybody, ya understand. It was okay . . . he was my friend. But I sure didn't want to go to jail. Ya see . . .

I was only doin' him a favor. I could drive. Yeah . . . a car. And he couldn't and he wanted to get a driver's license. And he asked me to take the test for him. Just pretend that I was him and take the test. So I said to him, cause he was my friend, I said to him that I would take his driving test for him. And I did. But I drove so good that the examiner got suspicious and checked my papers out and then my handwriting and next thing I knew I was in jail. For thirty days. My friend didn't even come to visit me or drop me a line. But it was cool, I guess. Not too bad, ya know. I've done time since . . . and remembering back . . . the first time was about like the last time. Though for a jive reason like that, I don't dig it too swell, man. My friend? . . . Well, he was sorry. But what could he do? They made it so that he could never get a license . . . ever. I wouldn't want to be in his shoes for shit, man. It only took me three years to get mine back. I was scared that they might mess with my license forever, ya know; but they didn't; I was kinda lucky; they only put me behind bars, Jim. . . . Ah, it was okay. I'm in good shape, ya know. Always been. Go to the gym all the time. If anybody had tried to get wise with me I'd ah knocked the punk out. . . . Look at this . . . ugh ugh. . . . See the form? How ya like it? . . . Ever see a jab like that? I been goin' down the gym since I was twelve. Was in the Golden Gloves too. Thought I might turn pro for a while. Might have been good, ya know. . . . Maybe even champ. . . . Yeah . . . yeah . . . yeah . . . yeah . . . you can't get a license with a police record.

YOUNG WEST INDIAN REVOLUTIONARY POET

No, mon. I am not a foreigner! I am Black like you and all Black men in America, Africa, the West Indies, where I was born, by the way, and the Third World. You should be fucken ashamed of yourself, mon. What you sayin' is completely and totally reactionary and counterrevolutionary. It is a crime what you are doing against Black people.

No lie. The reality of the situation is that you are very well mistaken about me and any other Black man that comes to you from another place. You're as bad as those stupid Africans, mon, who say that we are not the same as they because we were not born in Africa. You should not say these things, you should not think the way you do. It is wrong, mon. Yes, it is that I know it is wrong. You have no basis in fact or reason to have you say or express an idea or attitude as that. We are all Black and we are in the very same struggle. Our revolution is against the white man, mon. And since we have one common enemy, then we need, I mean it is vital that we unite together as Black people all over the world, mon, to take on the Western imperialist capitalistic colonial regimes. No more of this fucken foreigner bullshit! We are united in revolution as one people. I accept you as a Black man, even though you were born in America. And I am Black like you or my African brothers and my revolutionary brothers throughout the Afro-Asian sphere of recognition/dominance. Do you understand what I mean, mon?

CONFUSED AND LAZY

Took advantage of you? I don't know what you mean. Didn't you say that it was okay what I did when we talked about this the last time? I don't really understand what you mean. You've given me chances? And I've taken advantage of you? But I thought we had settled it. Look. You know the problems that I am having at home. And you know that it is wearing me mentally, emotionally and physically. You know that, don't you? Can't you understand? Good. But it gets in the way of what I have to do if I allow my personal life and problems to get in my way. No, you don't see. No, you don't. I never said that I would look after what I had to look after if I had emergencies to take care of. Of course I don't have daily emergencies. But the last several weeks I've had to neglect what I should be doing cause emergencies arise and problems exist and I can't stand the pressure of having to do what I should do and worrying about my problems too. I hope you have it all straight now. You fully understand that I never took advantage of your reason and naïveté, right? I'm sorry you're acting like this. Can't we talk? I have so much to tell you. No, of course I don't think you're the bad guy but you're misperceiving me wrongly. It's not at all like that. Can't you understand my point-of-view in this whole thing? There is a bit of confusion here, but it'll be all right and not harm us a bit. No, I am not trying to take advantage of your idealism. You believe me, don't you?

THE GENIUS

Yes, I am going to be one of the greatest ever. I can feel it. I know it. Don't ask me how or why. I just am. The feel, the taste, the flow that the vibrations make causes me to know. Everything is coming. Some coming faster than I can almost manage but I do and it is good good good. My life is more glowing. I can love better and more because my work is coming. No, going, rising gloriously. It is no wonder that I am convinced of my greatness. With the few examples of my brilliance that I have turned out there can be no mistake in anybody's mind, especially mine. There's nothing else to do than to get down to work. In ten years I may be approaching the end of my apprenticeship. With ten full years of constant work attempting to grow into and beyond my work there is no limit to the profound degree of insight my genius will have in shaping my work. All great artists have had to work through years of trial and error. Some without the barest amount of companionship and patronage. Some not becoming known in their lifetimes. I do not want to be discovered after death. My work will grow through the years in importance, naturally, and command great sums after my death, no doubt, but in actuality I want to reap many of the rewards that fame, success and power give to a man of such fantastic gifts, imagination and artistry as myself. It may seem a bit vain, my making these remarks and my being candid with you, but that is one of the secrets to my greatness: tell and show as much as you can stand. And be ruthless with yourself, on occasions, to uphold these standards. For only I can do what I can do. And what I can do is special, important and inspirational. There's only one me, but there will be thousands of imitators. That is some of the best types of flattery for my genius.

THE THEORIST

Yes, my brother, we are our fathers' sons. Our fathers' sons. And that is the only way it can be. That is how it happened. Our sperm, the seeds within us, represents life as our fathers' evolved seed that we have become; once sperm, a tadpole-like creature, minutely small, we swam and crawled up the ladder of life which is human evolution to stand here now, on two legs. We are a continuation of the evolutionary life process that goes on within us outside of us and in spite of us throughout our race of mankind. We are men, surely, but we are seed, sperm and hairless animal as well. We are father, sperm, child, embryo and son. We are the life/givers, life/containers and life/receivers. Our women, loved and cherished as they need to be, are not the bearers of life but the repositories of life on a specific plane, and then become the caretakers of that life until it matures and rises and goes on. Woman is merely a receptacle for the seed of life and a home for it, for a short while, until life is ready to move on. Her egg nourishes the seed, that tadpole-like thing which is called the sperm, and she is the fertile earth and incubator for life, that she is, and sustains that life through its evolutionary changes until it is ready to enter this world. And at that moment the father's seed enters the mother with all potential of knowledge, ability and racial characteristics. It enters life fully connected to its father through genetic transfer. So all that we have and receive we take from the moment of conception from our fathers, the life/givers, the passers-on of the seed of life, from the moment of conception whereby our fathers shoot their life into the fertile egg and life-nourishing areas of the mother and the magic transaction called life takes place, whereby the sperm splits into an embryonic organism, and our generation came to be on this plane of existence, also named life, stimulated by the natural life processes of the race, the family, the nation, our parents, the fathers and mothers of the Black man.

FRIED BRAINS

Hey . . . who you tellin' ta come 'mere? I ain't your puppy dog. I ain't supposed to be comin' to you whenever you whistle. I'm a girl, not a broad . . . and kinda fine. With a small, little waist . . . a nice butt and bowlegs. I'm short too. And I got a nice chest. So, watch how you talk to me, baby. Yeah, I know my hair's comin' out. It don't take to hot combs and irons. But it's the style, ain't it? In nineteen-fifty all us girls do our hair. What would we do with it if we didn't straighten it? I just don't know what I'm gonna do, man. If my hair keeps fallin' out like this. Maybe you'll buy me a wig, huh? Won't you do that for me? That'll fix me up swell . . . yeah, a wig . . . a blond one . . . oooooeeee . . . that would be nice. Honey, with the right clothes and a together front I'd be a knockout . . . but that takes dough, right, Joe? You got any do-re-me, sweet cake? You ain't? And I'm too black for a blond wig anyway. Hey, motherfucker, don't you call me black! . . . Sonna bitch! Who you think you are? . . . Awww, chump . . . I ain't gonna be your ole lady . . . or nothin' else. You don't even know how to talk to me or treat me. . . . You pussy! . . . Hey! . . . you better not hit me, nigger. You ain't nothin' . . . nothin' . . . and you never have been nothin' . . . and you ain't never gonna be nothin'. I don't

[176]

need you to buy me no wig. . . . If you don't like what my bald-ass head looks like, sucker, you can kiss my high-stacked black booty.

TRAPPED

Awwww, nigger . . . I don't want to do nothin' 'cept lay. Dig? Yeah, it's a drag, man. Everything's a drag. Can't find a gig . . . not the kind of job I'm lookin' for anyway. And this standin' on the corner is a drag, if you can dig where I'm comin' from, champ. Here I am . . . in my mid-twenties standin' on a corner without a dime in my pocket. It's a triangle . . . if you hip to that . . . the pool room . . . the corner bar on the other side of the street . . . and I'm holdin' down this corner here. That's about it. . . . Hey, what you been doin' lately? Don't see you much anymore. . . . Oh, you goin' a night school . . . and you work during the days. . . . So you don't swing out no more, huh? . . . That's too bad. . . . You don't mind it, huh? . . . Sounds like it would be a drag to me. Yeah . . . you all the time havin' to read a lot of books and to be on time and all that other stuff. . . . You don't like some of it yourself, huh? Well, I didn't think you did, man. That what you doin' sounds unnatural . . . at least to me, man. They tryin' to turn you into a punk, man. That's some faggot shit, ain't it? Sounds like you an old, half-dead dude already, man. . . . Yeah, why don't you cut it loose, man? . . . I would, if I was you. . . . What would you do? . . . Well, I don't know, man. . . . You could do what we usta always do. Stand on the corner here. Hang around the pool room. Hang out in the bar . . . or join the Army like some of the guys do. . . . I might have done that if I had a clean rap sheet. . . . But I'm into a heavy petty criminal thing, man. The Man is always ready to vamp on you and take you off 'round here or put you in the slammers . . . and a lot of things are goin' down, man. . . . The Mafia's startin' to lay some heavy drugs on the brothers up near the avenue.

. . . It's comin' down this way now. Whatever, man . . . you could find something to do . . . if you came back. . . . We could try together, bro.

WAITING

Gone, nigger. . . . I don't want you jivin' with me. . . . sheet . . . everytime I look around you sniffin' round me. What you think you are . . . a pimp, or somethin'? I already got an ole man. You know that, so what you hangin' round me fo'? Can't even get out my door or up the street before you tippin' over to me sayin': "Hey, baby. What's happenin'? What'cha doin' tonight, baby? Why don't we make the set?" See what I mean, man? That's jive you know. My ole man will be home soon. He's got only forty-three more days to serve on his sentence . . . and he'll be home . . . if he gets his good-time. . . . And you supposed to be his best friend, man. How you sound? That just ain't right. . . . Oh, stop it! You make me sick. . . . Always tellin' me how much you dig me. How much you want me. . . . Well, I know you want me . . . that's why you here, right? Right! Well, it ain't gonna do you no good. . . . I don't care how many drinks you buy . . . I don't care how sweet you talk . . . or what you promise me. . . . You just ain't bout to get nex' to me, Jim . . . you wastin' your time. . . . So get up off me before I holler or somethin', man. . . . You hear what I said, huh?

THE RAPPER

Brothers, we are slaves. Slaves in this moment of history. Nothing short of that, however we wish to disguise this fact. We are dependent. We suffer from repression. Worst, we are subservient. In fact, brothers, as I said before, we are slaves. And what I am calling for is a slave revolt. Yes, brothers, a slave revolt. An honest-to-god revolution. The time has come for us to throw off the shackles of the slavemasters. The time has come for us to rise up as men and rulers of our own destiny. The time has come for us to assume our roles on the world stage of revolution. No more will we stand for the degradation and humiliation of this living death. No more will we stand aside and watch our fellowmen, our women and children led into the confines of the oppressed. No more will we become accomplices to tyranny. For if one doesn't fight against this evil government with all resources at his command, whether it be hands, teeth and feet, then one is an accomplice to that evil. Yes, I say it now and I say it again, no more will we be tools of the evildoers and lynchers. Yes, lynchers, my brothers. No more will we aid him in his wars of genocide and imperialism, nor will we prove passive concerning his designs of colonialism. We will be new men or the very earth will shake with our rage and fury. We will be masters of our own or the skies will witness a holocaust of biblical proportions. We are slaves now, this moment in time, brothers, but let this moment end with this breath and let us unite as fearless revolutionaries in the pursuit of world liberation!

BEWILDERED

Wow, chief . . . my ole lady is somethin' else. She won't give me any pussy unless I go through gorilla changes with her, man. And this is what's so cold, brother. The broad's out to shoot me if I even stay out late. Yeah! For real! Shoot me! That's what she says . . . and that broad might be fo' real, man. I can't get next to how she thinks. She's uptight at me, dig? Been that way for more than a year. Somethin' I said or was supposed to have done, right? So she gets tight with her leg. Hardly no action. Don't want to give up much box. Only occasionally. Well, I might not look it, buddy-buddy, but I like my good steady snatch, see? Every night almost, unless somethin's wrong. And she ain't gettin' off nothin' without some static . . . and when it happens it's not the greatest experience of my career . . . if you know what

I mean. No heart on her part . . . if you can dig it. So I try to take it philosophical, ya know. We got these crumb crushers, and I ain't goin' nowhere as long as they there. I dig my crumbs, baby. So I start checkin' out some action . . . in a cool way, you understand? Nothin' serious . . . just somethin' fly to take a fling with. And I stay out a night or two . . . then WHAM! . . . just like that . . . she's on the scene like Bonnie and Clyde. . . . Pure show biz. . . . Could'a been a monster. So I'm wonderin' what goes on in her head, jack. Sure was cold . . . walkin' into my pad and havin' my ole lady tryin' ta jam me. And oh, yeah, friend . . . when I finally gets myself together and talks to her . . . she happens to tell me she borrowed the rod from you. Can you get to that?

HARLEM MOTHER

My boy Jimmie's away for the summer, you know. Just put him on the plane. . . . Went to Texas . . . visitin' his cousins. . . . My . . . my . . . took him less time to get there than it took me to get back home. . . . I came back from the airport on the subway. . . . Yeah . . . he called me soon as he got there. My phone was ringin' as I was climbin' the stairs. We live on the fifth floor . . . just around the corner on a Hundred and Thirty-Seventh. . . . He said he liked it. Just think of that . . . and he just got there. Probably wanted me to feel good and not to worry. . . . Hmmm . . . I'm really tired. Been standin' all day in the food line. . . . Yes, the food lines are back. Just like before when I was a little girl and they had the WPA. . . . But this time they give out food stamps . . . an you go around to the school and they give you food out of the basement. Lots of people were waitin' . . . for hours. It was terrible. The heat was so bad . . . and people was gettin' mad cause other people was tryin' to get in front of them and they had been there since morning. And we waited and waited. . . . And they ran out of food. . . . It was terrible. They knew how many food stamps they had given out . . . so they knew how much food they needed. But they ran out. And the people were mad. Most said that they wasn't comin' back to stand in the line. I don't blame them. I ain't gon' go back until nex' month. People talk about stealin' before they come back there and stand in the line all day in the heat and then don't get nothin'. I was scared for a minute. Thought there'd be some real trouble. I remember the riots, you know. . . . All of them since I was a girl here in Harlem. I know how it is. When the riots come there ain't no food at all. The police and Army won't let nothin' in 'cept whiskey and wine. Yeah, that's right. That's where most of the money is at in Harlem. In the bars and liquor stores on every corner. Nex' is the churches . . . but they don't count as much anymore. Powell lost and he's got his big ole church behind him . . . always did . . . but it don't count for nothin' no more. I don't even make Jimmie go, like my mother made me and my sisters and brothers go. Don't count fo' nothin' like it usta. . . . But I don't mind his comin' round here to the theater like he always does. Nawh . . . I ain't been in yet . . . but my boy comes . . . and he likes it. . . . Said he'd be back in time to see what you do nex' . . . You know . . . when anything happens they really protect the liquor. . . . You know . . . if people here in Harlem could stay away from liquor this would be a different place. Now wouldn't it? Wouldn't it? . . . You know it would. And now they talk so much about dope. . . . I don't even know what that stuff is but I know it's worse than that ole wine and I usta think that was the worse. . . . Lawd . . . I'm glad I could send my boy Jimmie away this summer.

BLACKNESS

August 3, 1970
Harlem

A SHORT PLAY FOR A SMALL THEATER

Lights up on a "little" theater. The space should be painted black—stage, walls, ceiling, seats, etc. No posters, no slogans, no liberation flags, etc.

For the purpose of this piece a three-sided seating arrangement should be best, with the last row in each section close enough for a tall actor to reach over and touch the occupant.

The place should not hold more than ninety people.

For this play the audience must be at least two thirds black. If more than a third of the audience that shows up is white they should be turned away to maintain the proper ratio.

Psychic music, incense, colored lights.

. . . at a small table a tall BLACK MAN *methodically applies colored face paint. The stripes and circles and dots make brilliant contrast to his dark skin.*

Upon completion of this ritual the BLACK MAN *carefully wipes his hands upon a towel, then places soft, black leather gloves upon his hands.* HE *then picks up a large hand gun and deliberately goes to each white person in the audience and shoots him in the face.*

If there is need HE *should unhurriedly reload as many times as necessary and complete his assignment.*

BLACKNESS

THE PLAY OF THE PLAY

Into a bare room the audience is ushered. The doors are locked from the outside.

Wide, bare walls. Some panels can be murals, or anything which will complement the lighting.

Lights down; colors and images (spots, light show, slides, 8- or 16-mm film projector, TV, etc.).

The floor is wired for sound. Every movement is picked up and broadcast over the sound system.

Unseen microphones are placed within the space in such a way that any sound that the audience makes is captured and broadcast throughout the room.

Unseen musicians begin to play; a heavy beat. Those of the audience who can, and have the inclination to, dance.

Poetry or compelling speeches can be broadcast into the room during the "performance."

Anything can be laid on the people that you wish through light, images, sound, movement and color.

BLACKNESS

December, 1970

[183]

The Theme Is Blackness

"The Corner" and Other Plays

by ED BULLINS

"Mr. Bullins, who could be called 'an angry young man,' is gifted with extraordinary imagination and ability. His play (*Goin' a Buffalo*) reflects the dramaturgy of Antonin Artaud yet brandishes the ideology of the current Black Left."

—WILLIAM COUCH, JR.,
New Black Playwright

In the brief introduction to these fifteen plays Ed Bullins, one of the nation's most celebrated playwrights, explicates the development of black theater from 1965 to 1970. He comments on such persons as Eldridge Cleaver, Bobby Seale, Imamu Amiri Baraka, and evaluates other playwrights. This makes for an interesting introduction, for rarely has a practicing playwright talked about so many of his contemporaries in so honest a fashion. Then, as if to say, "This is how it should be done," Bullins gives us fifteen plays that range from character studies to radio commercials. "The Corner" was produced at the New York Shakespeare Festival Public Theater to critical acclaim.

"He [Bullins] is, when writing 'at home,' a writer of extraordinary power and insight where one exhibited fault is a disappointing lack of range. Yet the depth to which this remarkably talented craftsman has gone in exploring the form and substance of Blackness as Blacks in America know it is more than a compensating factor."

—CLAYTON RILEY,
The New York Times

"Ed Bullins is quickly becoming not only the best Black playwright in the nation, but one of the most admired playwrights of any color."

—*The National Observer*

"Bullins is an emerging theatre poet in the tradition of Tennessee Williams, inspired and gorgeous."

—GOTTFRIED,
Women's Wear Daily

"[Bullins] is writing what could not have been written before him: the emotional history of his own era."

—*Look*